Surpassing Peace

Our Circumstances are Roadblocks,

Peace is Our Rescue

LINDA GOTTSCHALK

ISBN 979-8-88751-120-7 (paperback)
ISBN 979-8-88751-121-4 (digital)

Christian Faith Publishing
832 Park Avenue
Meadville, PA 16335
www.christianfaithpublishing.com

Unless otherwise stated, all Scripture references were taken from the New International Version of the Holy Bible.

Printed in the United States of America

Prelude

Our circumstances are roadblocks. Peace is our rescue.
Peace cannot be held by force. It can only
be present through surrender.

Have you experienced peace in your life? Each of us have a story, and that story lives inside and outside each of us. We wear our story like a raincoat for its protection. At times our story is likened to the wind dancing through the trees to capture the attention of those who look up. Dare we look up to see too and see God's story in us?

God has been writing his story in my life for over thirty years. He has painted for me a crazy, messy, beautiful canvas that begs me to pause often to reflect and remember. These times of pause remind me of the grace I have been given and how deeply I am loved. My canvas is colorful! It has been covered with the gift of peace that only surrender brings. What does your canvas look like? I hope it is colorful too. My desire for you and me is to live our colorful canvases out loud for the world to see the masterpieces they are.

I'm a church girl who loves Jesus most in her life. My life wasn't always defined this way. I lived a life by my own standards, which didn't always serve me well. Maybe you can relate. We all have our own stories. We have walked paths we shouldn't have. We've all been given more to carry than we should or could have. If you were that person who had a dream like childhood, bless you, my friend! You had a really good head start in this thing called life. If you didn't, you might still be working out your stuff in search for peace, and you might not be ready at all.

Don't shut this book just yet. Give this story a chance to speak to you. When we share our stuff, we have an opportunity to help others become more whole than they were yesterday. I would like to take this opportunity.

Have you lived a season in life that was *one you just couldn't make up*? One filled with trials that pushed you into unchartered waters that felt deep, too deep. This will always be a heavy, hard season.

I have heard it said that when things get rough, share it because it helps. Helps what? Good question. I believe when we unpack the hard stuff, we open our hearts and minds to healing and peace. Living our stories out loud is part of the great adventure we don't want to miss. What will we miss? We will miss the hidden blessings like diamonds in the rough. We will miss out on lessons to be learned and finding our purpose and passion.

I am going to do something new for me. I am going to journal my story, my circumstances, and my surrender to peace. It's risky because the hard stuff can sting like an open wound. There is freedom in giving oneself permission to share. Worth the risk? I think so. Have you ever journaled part of your story? If you have, I hope it took you on a beautiful journey. If you haven't, I pray this will be an encouragement and invitation to try something new too.

God's story in me isn't bigger or harder than yours; it's just mine. Sharing the circumstances of my hard season is not the purpose of my story. Our circumstances do not have to define us, but what God can do in our circumstances is worth not just holding it close to our hearts but to share with others.

God's Story through Me Begins Here

1997

It was January 2020. I was getting ready to go the Dominican Republic. My hubby, I, and our girls have been short long-term missionaries for thirty years and counting. We learned early on that we never want to do for others what they can do for themselves. People don't need big fancy houses and cars to get by, but people do need dignity to feel valued and a chance to believe in oneself. All people matter. My life has been transformed by the opportunity to live this mission life out loud. It's a "God-story" that runs deep into my soul and has launched me into a world that needs love so desperately.

While preparing for one of our short-term mission trips, I began to feel ill. I got a cough unlike anything I had ever experienced and wouldn't go away. I am a let's-go-get-'er-done kind of girl, but whatever this was wouldn't allow me to do my eleventh-hour push. If you are crazy like me, you understand that eleven-hour push. I finally went to the doctor. He said, "Maybe strep." Tested negative. Let's try influenzas A through B and whatever else. We were living our pre-COVID life. All testing was negative. The doctor sent me home to rest. I did, and in time, I was feeling mostly better; however, I never got my eleven-hour push back, but I still landed the first ten well.

March 2021 (I think). Dates and times are a bugger for me. You will understand. A new day and life for all of us was born. The birth of COVID-19. All our lives stopped in those few short days in March. We will never be the same. We instantly lost control of what we thought life was. Our future, our kids, our government, and life as we knew had been deconstructed. We have all heard of the domino effect. Well, this is what we were experiencing during this time.

God uses the hard for good. Sometimes we can't wrap our heads or hearts around this when crisis strikes. But him being God, he does use the most devastating things for good. We must come to a place to believe this or not. I believe it. I wonder if you do too.

In August 2020, we had planned a trip with our family to our daughters-in-law's nice, comfy cabin with all fun water stuff. It's a beautiful place to love my people and laugh a lot. Hubby and I decided to take a couple days before that trip began and have some honey time together. We went to Pictured Rocks, a beautiful place found in Michigan. I got this strange cough again right before we left and felt exhausted. No eleven-hour push.

I grabbed Advil and cough drops, and away we went. By then, a cough had been redefined in the COVID world. You best be careful coughing around people. A whole lot of crazy could happen. The human spirit was broken during this time. Fear is real and can be devastating. One thing was for certain: the COVID crisis had changed the fingerprint of this world.

I was feeling worse, but we wanted to go on a cool yacht sunset ride. We sat in the back so I could cough off the back of the boat. Fun times. The cool breeze felt good on my fever. I got some amazing pictures. People were not okay with my condition. I think I ruined their evening. To be kind, we gave up our family trip and went home. I tested negative but was really sick. The end of summer was upon us, and I didn't want to miss those last days of August gathering with friends; so I was creative in how I could embrace those last days. I got better, but I never got rid of this little cough.

People are my passion. I am a retired hairdresser. I still cut a bit of hair in my house because I know that curbing my passion brings discontentment. Do you have a passion? I hope you do. Chase after it and indulge in it. Make it what you get lost in. You will learn so much about yourself. Don't be afraid to step into unchartered waters to reach your potential and passion. Take the risk. It's worth the sweaty palms it brings. You will never regret making your passion purposeful. Go get it! (On a side note, don't care what others say. Check your character and conquer it.)

Because I still felt funky sometimes, as a trustworthy hairdresser, I would test every time I had a client. Many negative tests made my clients and myself happy. We wore our masks and giggled as I did my magic around the funky little masks. We found humor in the hard things.

When COVID-19 hit, our world was torn into shreds. I didn't want to isolate. It would have taken me into a deep, dark place. I needed to learn how to navigate in restricted spaces like the rest of the world around me. I found a new gig. Well, that's not really accurate. God gave me a new assignment, and I was thrilled.

God just knows what we need when we need it. This new mission kept me passionate for people. I got involved with our local homeless shelter and our sober living rescue in our city. The homeless people aren't especially worried about restricted areas. A city bridge is pretty big. When all you have is a backpack and a piece of cardboard, you aren't taking up too much space. A homeless friend once told me that living in wide-open spaces means freedom. He had a point to ponder.

For this next part of the story to make sense, I have to take you back a couple years. Stay with me. We were watching the nightly news, and a high school friend's face popped up on the screen as missing. If anyone saw him, they were to report it. It was John. This hit me hard, a mysterious hard. I was shaken but didn't really understand. It twirled me all the way back to the good times John and I shared. He was like a brother I never had.

We were close back then in those high school years. Life happens; we grow up and go on to make our own ways. I told my hubby that night, "If John is ever found and if I ever see him, I need to know his story."

Our busy lives carried on. We were driving somewhere, and there he was. It was John on a bike. He looked different, way different. He was a mess. Guess what? We didn't stop. I can hardly write those words. That bore a hole right into my gut. Learn from me. Stop and follow those nudges. But God…God is faithful and in the details. Let me tell you about my Jesus. He is a God of second chances. He makes a way even when we mess it all up.

Hubby and I were off-loading food donations at the mission one day. I looked up the ramp, and there he was. I was staring at John but was not quite sure because it's been thirty years since we talked. He was nervous, I could tell. You would be too, the way I was staring him down. So not polite. I walked up to him and spoke, "John."

He said, "Linda," in a garbled way.

I grabbed him and hugged him and then felt a bit like, *Why did you just do that?* I guess because my Jesus said so. I couldn't understand him but tried my best to catch up. I told him I would like to see him again. He wanted that too. I was excited but walked away a little bit sad because he was drunk. No judgement, but it would adjust this newfound relationship. John would become so much more than I could ever imagine. Today I still sit in this mystery of a very intentional purposeful love.

Did I mention God is in the details? If we are walking through this life in awareness, we will see God's fingerprint on everything.

Days, weeks, maybe months go by; I don't remember. We were delivering pizzas on Friday night to the gazebo where the homeless gathered to party. It was a sketchy place to be, but it was where we knew God wanted us to be. It was getting to be fall, and winter was soon to be. Hubby and I brought clothes and the critical needs for the homeless looking to a cold winter ahead. We came to enjoy our community of homeless friends, to love them, and to remind them that they matter. Two communities colliding as they should. We are all just people with a story. We were there to learn about theirs.

I turned around, and there was John. He said his bike got stolen, so he was on foot. We tried to talk. I could tell he wanted to. We moved off to the side, and he said he found out that day he had cancer, throat cancer. He wasn't drunk. I assumed he was all along, and I was so wrong. I felt sick for a minute. I learned a big lesson in that moment. Don't assume. Learn from me, okay?

I cried and hugged him again. This time I didn't wonder why. He spoke, "I am going to fight hard, Linda."

I said, "Can I help you fight?"

A tear fell from his eye. He said, "No one has cared for me like this." We hugged again and then began getting our plan with the doctors. I learned so much about the homeless and how to get help for them. How to be the hand to hold when people stare in the waiting room. Don't stare; care instead.

Homeless people don't always smell the best, and that is okay. I learned how to be his voice because he no longer had one. I learned to wipe the sweat from his brow that poured out from unbearable pain. I learned to look into his eyes a lot. It was there. I began to see more and more of his story.

John lived in a homeless shelter that wasn't setup for his desperate situation. We had to find a way to get him to a place where he could climb the big mountain ahead of him in peace. That is how he could fight the right fight: with our help.

Desperate situations feel impossible. They feel impossible to manage and impossible to see a fix. I am reminded in these hard times that God is in control and has our circumstance all worked out. We just have to wait for his next best thing because God will reveal it. We have much to learn in the wait.

Just weeks before this difficult news with John, I had started volunteering at the sober living center. It was an all-men facility where men came to live and grow through programing to one day send them back to the streets healthy and equip to find their passions too. I asked the director if John could have a room to stay in. We would find a way to pay his way, and we would care for him regarding appointments and any needs he might have. They agreed. This would be God's reveal to the next best thing for John.

Never be afraid to step out and ask hard questions even when you don't have the answers. Take the risk. Trust your heart and step out into the unknown prepared for the challenge. It's part of the great adventure!

John lived in his truck with flat tires mostly because the shelter wasn't an environment for his condition, and he was always a shy and private guy. His truck had to leave when he left to move into the sober living center. A big complicated job that needed to be done quickly. Who owned this truck? Is it paid for? His life was piled high from window-to-window, filled to the brim. Let that sink in. He actually had a pretty cool little set up. I loved his DVD player rigged up. He was creative. It was humbling to clean up his life from the truck. We got to look into year by year of what happens when you lose your way.

John came out as we were finishing up his truck. I will never forget this. It was like yesterday. He looked terrible. He said his stomach hurt so bad. It was Thanksgiving Day. At this point he had a feeding tube placed because the cancerous tumor in his throat was too big to do surgery. We knew this stage 4 cancer was deadly, but he wanted to fight. So we were fighting with hope. Miracles are real even today! Do we believe it?

I told him he had infection in his tube, so off to the hospital we went. Remember, it's COVID, and no one is allowed to stay in the hospital with their people. I was a bit mad but understood the reasonable rule. I told the people at the desk he couldn't really talk, and he was too weak to write. They told me to wait outside.

Within ten minutes, they were calling me and having me come to be his spokesperson. Peace came over me like a river in this moment. I had grown a bit protective over my friend. I think they saw this in my eyes.

The surgeons had John ready for surgery. His situation was critical. The doctors needed me to help John understand the circumstance he was in, his big roadblock. I went to John and took his hand. Our eyes met in a very deep way. Tears rolled from both our eyes. I asked John if he understood what the doctors were saying. He pulled me close and said yes in his garbled way. Somehow we learned how to communicate our own way.

We did a lot of talking with our eyes. It's difficult to write this because it runs deeper than words. The doctors needed his consent. They wheeled him into the surgery room. They took me in with him. It felt so cold, strange, and eerily quiet in there. I had to sign his papers there in that place. I felt I was signing him off. Gut-wrenching—that is what that is.

He waved me over and pulled me in and spoke, "Go home. You did enough."

I looked at him as my adrenalin rose up. I spoke, "Oh no, that is not how this goes. *We* came to fight. You are going to fight from where you are, and I am going to fight on my knees over there. I will not leave you."

He cried and turned away. I walked away.

The doctor took me somewhere; I have no idea where. I had been in this hospital many times, but not during COVID at midnight where the halls are completely empty—no people, no nothing. Silence. Eerie. I sat there in a big funk. I just talked to my Jesus. So many songs and scriptures flooded my mind. It was a story of its own that felt went on forever.

I found myself smiling and then thinking there is no place like home until you fall into the arms of Jesus. This would be a good night if that could be for John. No more pain and suffering. No more loneliness and sadness and looking at the stars.

I remembered calling him often at night when he was on the streets and say, "Hey, buddy, just calling to see where you are tonight and if you are okay."

He wouldn't usually answer for his own reasons, but when he would, he would often say, "Linda, I'm under the stars, and they are beautiful tonight."

I would then go sit on my beautiful deck and speak, "Yes, John, they are." That's two worlds colliding right there. I would say goodnight and sit peacefully awhile in wonder. And that would be that. Surreal.

The surgeon came walking toward me. I was braced for the news. I was ready for either after my sweet talk with Jesus. He said, "John is alive by a miracle only. He is a very sick man. It will be day by day." The surgeon said, "You can go home now."

I said, "Okay, but could I have John's clothes?"

He looked at me, and then he looked at me again and said, "Is this all he has?"

To that I said, "Pretty much." His truck house had been eliminated at this point. He got me the clothes and handed them to me. He was waiting for me to go, and I spoke, "I don't know where I am."

We both laughed, and he said, "Let me walk to your car." I told him he didn't have to do that, but to just point me in the right direction. He laughed and said, "It's a longer walk than what you think."

To that, he asked me where I parked, and I spoke, "I don't know because I don't know where I am." We both burst out in laughter. He said we would figure it out. On the walk, it was mostly awkward. I am not used to a surgeon walking me to my car holding a bag of a homeless man's clothes. I was on an adventure. They aren't always comfortable.

We were strangers, but it didn't feel like it; and we were both very tired for different reasons. He said to me, looking straight ahead, "I can't ask too much, but why do you do this?" Before I could answer, he said, "Is he your brother, and is he homeless?"

I smiled and said, "He's my friend like a brother. He's homeless, and I do this because I love him."

To that, he said, "This is some kind of love." In my mind, I said, *Thank you, Jesus, my sweet Jesus.* We kept walking. He handed me John's bag of clothes, and I said, "Happy Thanksgiving." I wonder what he was thinking on his walk back. I still think of him today. He was a good man who, I think, learned a lot that Thanksgiving night.

We are only strangers for a moment with those we reach out to. Don't ever waste a moment to love the unexpected deeply. Let it be awkward. Let it take you so far out of your comfort zone that you can't understand it. Don't try. Let it be surreal because that is often where real happens.

John would be in the hospital recovering and resting. I would be very busy getting his new space ready for him at the sober living center. It would be set up for his comfort and recovery in mind. It was so nice. John would be off the streets. I asked God to fill the space with a peace for John he had never experienced before. I sat on his cozy bed and felt it, that deep peace. As I sat in his room, I thought about if he might miss the stars. I decided that day that we would take a drive as often as he liked to sit and gaze upon them.

This cough would become my circumstance and roadblock! Honestly, I was furious this time. Furious. This church girl who loves Jesus had some strong words with her Father. I could hear my Lord say, *My beloved, my thoughts are not your thoughts. You can't see what I can. It wouldn't be right. It wouldn't in your time. It's all in my time.* Deep breath and surrender. This is what our Father patiently waits for. Oh, I wanted to stomp my feet and tell God how it should go, but peace and pride don't live together.

My cough meant I couldn't be with John, so my sweet hubby and pastor friend picked John up from the hospital. I sent his clean bag of clothes with them. I took the cigarettes and lighter out of his pocket but left his couple of dollars he had. The pastor talked about John's relationship with the Lord. Did he have one? I never asked him, that hard Thanksgiving night. I could have felt guilty for this, but there was a reason I didn't. Some things will always be a mystery to us, but never to God. When we can trust like this, the great adventure is greater.

They met John and his smile. When hubby told me this, I knew he was still in the fight. He felt victory in that smile; I know he did in spite of that horrible Thanksgiving night. He was thankful, and so was I. John wanted to stop at the gas station. Hubby thought that was odd but said it would be okay. He went in, and sure enough, out he walks with a pack of cigarettes and a lighter.

I am still shaking my head…at myself. If I were him, might I still want to smoke? Heck yes! So who was I to take that away from him? More for me to learn. I loved John's stubborn side. I still wonder to this day, when he reached in his pocket for his cigarettes, what he said. I can only imagine. (I'm laughing.)

The door opened to what would be John's new home. He went to the bed, sat down, and looked around. How I longed to be there, but I wasn't supposed to be. God's story in my life has taught me that to obey is to draw one step closer to God. When we release our will, and trust his, we are positioning ourselves into the glory of God. It's a blessing when we can see this world from God's view.

Hubby told me everything, every last look and detail. John felt the peace that had filled his space. Hubby said that he felt pulled to move toward John. He put his hand on his shoulder and told John he couldn't leave without asking him something. He asked John if he knew Jesus as his personal savior.

John looked up at him and gave him a big smile, and hubby leaned in. John said, "August." I found a used Bible in his truck. I had placed it next to his bed. I later found out that his daughter gave him that Bible. I know he cherished it. Hubby and Pastor prayed and left. I was so happy that he was safe. He was in the quietness of his space filled with peace in a hard circumstance.

I got my COVID-19 results back Sunday morning. *Negative!* I was so happy and was feeling much better. I told hubby I was going to watch a DVD with John. I called him to let him know I was coming. He didn't answer. I was sure he was out having a cigarette. He gave up all his addictions except that one. I told hubby I would just go and surprise him. I got to his room and was walking on a cloud. It would finally be our time.

Let these anxious moments of joy overwhelm you. Don't stop them. We need to experience this kind of joy. Do not miss those moments. There is so much raw love that flows from these places.

I could barely contain myself.

His door was opened a little. I stepped back and thought, *Hmm, that is weird.* But then maybe not; he was homeless. Where he lived, there were no doors, and maybe the door made him feel closed in. A perspective to ponder for a bit. I was crawling out of my skin to spend time with John. I called out for him. I was just about to turn around to check the smoking area but decided to push the door open a bit more. He was laying on his comfy bed so still. Then something wasn't right. I sensed it. I called his name again, and he didn't answer or move. No.

I got sick in that moment because I knew. I went and got the resident manager and told him to come with me because I thought John was dead. We both walked in, and John was gone. He was laying with his hands crossed as if he were in a coffin, and his face was so peaceful. I reached down and touched his hands. They were cold, but that's okay; he wasn't there. He was in the arms of Jesus. He was home, really home, finally. I smiled through the tears. I don't know how to unwind those minutes we stood there in silence. So I won't. There was a deep peace that filled his room. I felt oddly grateful in spite of it all.

This was now the beginning of December. How do you plan a funeral for a homeless man of ten years? More to learn for sure. Our church was so kind to have John's homegoing celebration to be there. We stored his truck house stuff in our garage until his family could come and go through his things. It was a small number of things. You don't need much to live on the street.

John's daughters came to our home to not only go through their father's things but to see into the life of their homeless father. You can't unsee these tender moments and can't fill the deep dark empty hole in their hearts. I felt helpless. Regardless of a father's choices, a little girl still longs to crawl up on her daddy's lap. That wouldn't be on this side of heaven. This was a brokenness that filled my garage that only the Lord could fix.

There are no words to fill a broken space like that. I learned some very valuable things that day. We can meet people in their brokenness and give them permission to feel the gravity of their pain. I am a mom, and my heart broke watching them hold dusty books Dad liked to read and weep. These beautifully broken daughters had to walk this path. I think we all do. It would be the beginning to their healing, and they would have to do it their own way. I failed to mention, these now-grown women had not seen their father in more than ten years.

They had to come to this place in order to realize that it was their Abba Father that would receive them and hold them until their hearts could heal. They needed to know that this Father will never leave nor forsake them. They needed to feel a deep sense of love and peace that comes from Jesus. I will never be the same. I know they won't either. A bond was built that day that will never be broken.

When we watch someone suffer this deep sorrow, let's always give them a big space to come undone. Let's give them permission to release their pain. Let's always be there to love them in their mourning. Let's give them a safe place to land. Let's be available to be the ones who can lead them to the Father's arms where peace and healing happen. This is love in its rawest form.

It was a couple of days before the funeral. And guess what? I wasn't feeling well…again. I got sick within hours with a high fever, and my cough was back. You really can't make this stuff up. This life can feel very unfair. I was feeling the heavy weight of this. This was surreal. I would be unable to attend the funeral. I wanted so much to be there. I wasn't supposed to be there for reasons I didn't need to know.

Life's interruptions can be really difficult. Our circumstances become big obstacles. If we long for peace in these hard places, we need to see our difficult times as divine interventions instead. We will find peace in this place.

I thought John's daughters would need me. I felt responsible. Oh, me of little faith. I was broken and needed closure and was certain I knew the only way. Oh me, wanting to have it my way. To be still in these moments takes something far bigger than ourselves. I am so grateful for the Holy Spirit that indwells me today. I laid in my bed receiving, a peace in spite of my longing.

I would have ruined what God has intended for good. No one needed me. They all needed my sweet Jesus to fill their hearts. Another beautifully broken day of lessons learned for me as I lay in my bed.

Do you believe God ordains our every day? I do.

God ordained this very special going-home service for John. Our pastor friend who brought John from the hospital was supposed to meet John because he would be the one to greet John's family and look into their eyes to most importantly tell them, without a shadow of a doubt, John was with Jesus. This wasn't by chance. In God's economy, there isn't "by chance"; it's "by God."

We can learn a lot of very important things about a homeless man in just a short time. What they have is little, but what they lived was a lot. Right or wrong, good or bad, happy or hard, John lived his story his way. Today would be the day his estranged family would be able to get a glimpse of peace in their brokenness looking into the pastor's eyes.

God uses the hard for good always, and he was laying out his plan. We won't always see it, or we might not understand. Perhaps if we did in the here and now, we couldn't handle it with our limited ways, or we might miss the message altogether.

John's family was broken; his family was a mess and in turmoil. It might explain part of John's story and his exit to the streets. We all have a family story, don't we? It was hard gathering his people for the funeral because none of them had seen John for many years, and what they remember was painful. Blame was pointed to every direction. Pain can unleash unhealthy behaviors. Funerals like this are quick and over and, frankly, so sad.

But God had something waiting for each of John's family. The funeral lasted two hours! This is the grace of God! God brought them together for his purpose: to bring peace and healing. They mourned together, they forgave each other, and they gave up bitterness and blame. Walls came down.

God had a plan for me on that day too. I learned a big lesson from these broken people. Sometimes we have to get out of the way so others can see and feel the hand of God change their hearts. God handpicks who he will use to reach others in their deepest darkest place. It won't always be me or you. I needed to learn this.

On December 12, I was very sick still. I had a high—too high—fever, and it was time to go into the emergency care. They gave me medicine and sent me home. Two days later, I sat up and unable to breathe. Back to the ER, dressed up in jammies and slippers.

My hubby and I gave each other a look; I tried to not see when he dropped me off. I had to go on alone due to COVID protocol. It felt very uneasy. I was very sick, and I knew it. Something inside me was fading away. I lost my person if that makes sense. A bad CT scan in COVID season isn't good. I had the killing cocktail. My journey was about to begin.

I was so blessed to be that church girl who loved Jesus most. He was my security, my peace, and my joy in the days to come.

I would spend the next ten days in the hospital with dying lingering in my mind. I could sense, in a surreal way, what was happening when I walked through those doors on that day. I was flooded with an odd sense of quiet. I checked in at the nurse station as if it was slow motion ordering a to-go order at Chipotle. Strange, huh? Very strange.

These next ten days would be lived in the raw and filled with a sweet peace in the midst of chaos. These days would become medically complicated. There would be real trauma that gripped me. There would be crazy joy, and yes, humor too.

When dying is a real possibility, what should one expect? What does one hope for? What does one think about? I was about to find out. If you have been in this sacred place, you have much to offer to others. Sharing my story is to share hope, to share peace, and yes, to share humor in the hard.

I am a medical mystery, so they didn't know how to treat me. I was on a *lot* of medication, and not one of them was working. With each day, I was losing the fight. In the midst of trying this and trying that, I would watch the staff work tiredly. I was not afraid. They sensed my peace and quiet, and honored this precious time.

My precious hubby was in crisis as much as I was. Helpless but not hopeless. He is a church boy who loves Jesus, so he clung to hope from afar. I cannot imagine sitting in a very quiet house in the waiting and not being able to help. This puts most men in a very difficult place. They are masters of fixing things for their brides. I know his heart was broken sitting alone in our home…waiting. This would be a huge burden for me. I want to make this better for him today, but it's not possible. Our healing process and paths are different. After it all, I asked my hubby what he did while he waited. He told me he did all the things that I would do in the house. He said he kept his mind busy and on me. My precious husband.

My hubby would check in daily at 10:00 a.m. because that is when the doctor came in. I don't recall those days. I'm glad he was able to get information. My daughters would call daily and want to talk to their mama. I don't remember much of our conversations, and writing this doesn't come without tears. My babies, how helpless and how sad for them. I couldn't be strong for them when they needed me most. This has left a hard-lasting effect on them, on me, on all of us.

I remember trying to write them a letter and couldn't because I was too weak. This was too heavy to carry. I slipped over that edge. I believe this would be the time I surrendered to the fight in my journey. I wasn't afraid. There was nothing to be afraid of. Peace filled my heart and mind and the space I was in.

With each day, I was feeling more and more like a mere shell. Medically speaking, my body was giving up its sustainable function.

Trauma. Now this is something that is messy. I won't go into the details, but things didn't always go well in the hospital; and I was alone. I didn't have a familiar hand to hold when this went wrong and when things failed. I didn't have someone to push the button for me when I couldn't do it for myself. I *hate* needles, and when you are dying, your veins don't like to be poked. One attempt included twenty-plus tries throughout my whole body to find a vein so they could put me to sleep for biopsies. Trauma is real. If you hate needles, you are feeling me here. I remember lying there and surrendering to that fight too. Someone asked me if I am still afraid of needles. Yes, I am not only afraid of them: I am mad at them.

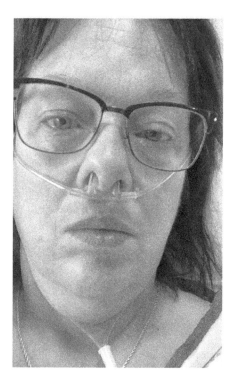

Trauma invades you while you are unaware. It happens *to* you. It comes without warning, and it affects you. You don't get over or move on from trauma. If you do the work, you bring it with you in a safe way as you live day-to-day.

Every day would begin at 10:00 a.m. to catch the doctors, which was for my hubby only. You see, I was very busy each day. I was fixated on the clock on the wall in front of my bed. For ten days...ten days fixated on a clock! Why? I have no clue! I remember this clearly but thinking it to be normal. Clearly not normal. I never took my eyes from it. The nurses had reason to be concerned. Trauma is tricky and doesn't explain itself well.

Humor. Crazy things happen when you are alone and determined in a challenged state of being. I am in no way, absolutely no way, making light of this serious reality; but I have learned you had better find humor in the hard, or depression and despair will cripple you and your healing ability.

As I was dying, my body craved salt in a big way. I wasn't able to put two and two together. I would order salt packets from the cafeteria and pour them down one by one. I remember having a funny picture in mind, like a chipmunk squirreling away nuts. I giggled. I needed to wash my hair. Why? That's a good question.

Where I was going didn't really matter. I remember washing my hair in the bathroom sink because the staff was busy. I recall laughing and giving the soap container a thumbs-up because it was antibacterial. Funny, but not really. Guess you had to be dying. The nurse would ask me if my feet were always so puffy.

I recall looking down at them and just telling her it was probably because I'm fat. She gave me a quirky look, and I smiled. Because my mind was affected and my brain was damaged, she would ask me the neurological questions. If you have been here, you know them. What's your name? Really? What year is it and so forth?

After day two of this, I asked her if I could ask her a question. She said, "Sure, ask me."

I said, "Do you think I am crazy?" She gave me that quirky look again. I told her I thought I was a little crazy so we could stop with the questions. My poor nurse.

I remember always admiring my nurse's hair. She was a beautiful Black woman. I sensed she had the peace I spoke of too. I loved having her in my space. She was supposed to be there. We rarely spoke, but she was there for all the right reasons.

That was a profound example to me that the Lord provides people you are in need of for just the right reasons that are clear, even if unspoken. Some really big and necessary things do not require words.

It was Christmas eve afternoon. I remember looking out my hospital window and seeing people in the blowing snow standing outside their loved one's hospital window. This happened a lot during the COVID crisis. Do you remember watching this on TV? It was in real time for me. I was experiencing this family from my bed. They were having Christmas the best and most loving way they knew how. I would watch them move their faces close to the window, hands as if they were reaching in.

The kids were playing in the snow. A mom was keeping the wind from her babies' face. I remember feeling their conflict too. What a blessing to be there, but what a tragedy too. Trauma. I wonder where they all are today. Hubby Facetimed, and I remember telling him all about it. I had incredible joy as I shared from afar with that desperate family on Christmas Eve.

The doctor came in at some point here and told us there was really nothing more they could do, and that my body was tired; but it would be my body now that had to fight. My doctor was masked. All I could see were his eyes.

I remember looking down and twirling my blanket between my fingers. This was a defining moment in my life. There is no more to say or to do. All control stripped away. I looked up and locked onto my doctor's eyes. He was stuck between sadness and emptiness. I could tell he had seen too much, and I wasn't his first rodeo. His eyes drew far away. I wouldn't let his eyes go and just said, "It's okay. It will be okay." My heart was so broken for him. He looked hard into my eyes one more time and walked away.

The next moments in time are too private to be able to express the love that was poured out between my precious husband who was waiting for me on FaceTime. It's wasn't like in the movies. It was quiet. Our eyes did a lot of the talking. I recall saying, "I am not exactly sure what the doctor means, but I think I know." My hubby just shook his head yes.

Love was in the air, in our eyes, in our souls, in our hearts that would never be taken from us even if this would be the last time our eyes met on this side of heaven. Oh, oh, *oh* how I longed to reach out and touch his cheek and lay down on his chest for a little awhile. I wanted to just touch him, to smell him. I closed my eyes, and we reminded each other how much love we got to share together as best friends. How do you end that conversation? We didn't know how.

I was invited to spend that Christmas eve in the most surreal and supernatural way with my Jesus. He was there in spirit. I had been suffering extreme pain, especially in the evenings. I hadn't taken pain medication that night. My pain…was gone. My body was light as a feather. I remember straightening my covers and feeling for my legs because I thought they were gone. I recall thinking, *They feel so good*. No more pain. My headache and chest pain were gone. My body was in a state of relaxation I have never experienced. Add this to the peace I had been given. I likened to the stairway to heaven. I exhaled with a big breath I had not done for days. No words will capture this reality I was in.

In that moment, I looked down, and I had crossed one hand over the other on my lap. I gasped and then just sat there and stared at my hands neatly laid on my lap. They were just like John's hands when I walked into his room to find him dead. It's crazy the odd things that go on when you are no longer in control, when full surrender has taken place. In that moment, my future felt very real. I laid my head back and thought, *Wow, this is it*. I wanted to hold onto the feeling in that moment. Peace, my friends, peace like I can't speak.

I was getting tired. My husband and my baby girls flashed through my mind. Our lives, our laughter, our long talks and walks. Our struggles and our victories. Being present when my babies had their babies. The giggle fits my hubby and I would have and couldn't stop. We lived life out loud, played hard, and loved deeply. That was too much to take in so quickly. I felt panic replace my peace, and a deep, devastating sadness overtook me. I was undone.

I knew I dare not ask the Lord for anything because the gift of peace was more than enough. But I had to and could not contain myself. I asked my sweet Jesus if he might take away this sadness I was feeling because I could not carry it. He spoke to my spirit in such a gentle way it paralyzed me. His spirit spoke the words, *No, my sweet child, I will not take away this sadness, because, beloved, this is love*. I laid back, tears flowing from my face, and whispered yes; and I drifted off.

22

It's Christmas morning. A very different Christmas morning. I woke up. My first thought, *This isn't heaven, and this isn't hell. I must be alive.* Of *all* things to think! That falls somewhere in between humor and trauma. Whatever it was, I was taken back and wide-awake. My hubby was on FaceTime. Our eyes met. It was a long stare I will never forget. It was all very surreal.

The doctor came in at this point and said, "Good morning!" I am still trying to process this new day. He said, "How do you feel?"

In some kind of funky alert state, I say, "Better, I think." I remember being so awake, and the room was so bright. It was so fresh. Something was different in the air.

He wanted to listen to my lungs. I noticed my annoying oxygen forklike thingy wasn't in my nose. He stepped back and said, "Your lungs have cleared up drastically." His eyes were very wide.

Here comes some amazing humor. Doctor didn't know hubby was on FaceTime. When the doctor said my lungs were cleared up, my hubby yelled tearfully loud, "Praise the Lord!"

The doctor said, "What was that"? (I was laughing so hard. You had to be there).

I said, "Oh, that is my hubby. He is happy." The doctor went on to explain that he couldn't explain. I said, "It's okay." I told him I didn't know where he was regarding faith, but I knew exactly what took place that Christmas eve night. He was stunned and unsure but decided it was a new day, and I was going to live.

I had experienced a miracle. Twelve hours ago, I was dying and knew it; I am now alive and healed. What does one do with this? I still don't know for sure. One might think there would be this emotionally charged change in one's life. Perhaps there has been for some. For me, it continues to be surreal, as I live differently now in the changes he did in me. I live today differently yet the same. It's a bit conflicting.

Things that mattered before no longer do. Some I miss, and some I rejoice in. I no longer have the need to get everything done like a crazy lady. I remember the old me and sometimes want to get back there to make sure everything is tidy and organized in my life, but God clearly saw that as a roadblock and is now asking me to live differently. I am getting used to it. I have never been an angry person, but things could get me fired up.

That is gone, and I rejoice over this. I just love people today. This is quite amazing. I recall telling my husband I was coming home a different person, and I did. It's surreal but very real.

Okay, here it is: one of the special moments I have been waiting to share. It's Christmas day, or the next day; I can't remember because I now have brain damage. I am feeling weak but was much better. I haven't gotten out of bed in five days.

The sun is going down, and I am going to order some hospital food. (It's good, by the way). I see something out of the corner of my eye. Some of my family that could be there were at my window. They're faces plastered, and hands pressing through the glass. My people! They brought love letters to share their hearts through the window. Our eyes met; I got out of the bed and walked to them. Our eyes met one by one. There is no greater love.

I imagined it to be like the day my Jesus comes back for me to bring me home.

I was home in my bed, lying on my hubby's chest within twenty-four hours—healed. Miracles do happen. Yes, they do. My miracle wasn't a movie miracle. It was God saying, *I am not finished with you yet, so put those big girl pants back on and get on with this life I have given you.* And that was enough. I was ready.

I was given a miracle, praise the Lord, but I still had a mountain to climb. These three rounds of COVID did me in. The high fever and low oxygen left me with some brain damage. I have spent the last eighteen months working hard to get my marbles in order again and getting my life back on track, as many others are. It's a process and, I will not lie, a very hard one. I am not who I was and may never be that girl again, but that is okay. Remember about the humor in the hard? Chase after it!

Heck, It's kind of fun. I lost half of my hair during this COVID crisis. It came back curly! I am now a curly haired lady. Hubby is loving his new wife. My new nickname is Covidhead because of my sometimes-scrambled brain. Everyone should have a hubby like mine. He is the best of the best.

I was a busy, type A, get-'er-done girl. I was capable too. I could multitask like a magician. I was hard to keep up with. My brain was affected by the virus. There is a significant glitch in the area of time. Type A people thrive on time and schedules. I no longer had that connection in my brain. Talk about an interruption! Time was something I no longer knew. Think about that with a get-'er-done mindset.

Torture. I can't help but giggle a little and say, "Duh, if you stared at a clock for ten days, you might get stuck too!" There is some humor in the hard. What was with that darn clock thing? I may never know. I am coming along well. I am making great strides in my recovery, and you know what? I live different. I really like this lady I have become. I like her a lot. She is taking in the time she has left in a very intentional way. She loves life in this new way. It's a new and great adventure with her Jesus. Divine interventions can take us places we could never imagine.

I am still that church girl who loves her sweet Jesus most.

I am sitting here today taking in this journaling. It's been two years of dealing with my divine interventions. It's been a long two years that has turned out to be very little about my COVID circumstance, but how profoundly I grew and learned so much about peace through my brokenness and trials. My desire was to share with you how each of our circumstances can be filled to the brim with peace and divine goodness in the midst of the hard.

Guess what? Six days ago, I got a bit of a scratchy throat. Thank the Lord, *not the cough!* I wasn't worried about it because it's spring, and I have allergies; so I was just nursing it along. Hubby took off for our daughter's house to help them with a project. My sore throat turned a bad corner fast. The pain returned, and I started to feel that same way again. Within two days, I was in the ER again. Like I said, you can't even make this stuff up.

I am now very familiar with the not-so-fun ER format. They gave me the good medicine for my pain. I laid back and felt somewhat comfy for the first time in a couple of days. I opened my eyes slightly, and there it was. *The clock.* I laughed, and then I didn't. I saw a chair next to the clock. I so wanted to get on that chair and rip that clock off the wall. I laid down and realized if I hadn't had my IV in, I would have done that. I scared myself with that thought, because then they would have taken me to a different hospital because they don't know my story. I laid back again and realized our stories really never end; we just add to them.

At that moment, they flung the door open, and my doctor said, "Well, it's official. You have COVID."

I couldn't laugh, but instead I said to myself, *Straighten your crown, queen. You got this.* I am recovering from home this time with oxygen isolated from my hubby. Just knowing he is there makes me melt. A huge blessing. I don't know what's next; I just know to expect another great adventure.

I am going to be real and transparent and honest. This is a lot. If I made this sound easy, it has not been easy. It has turned my world upside down. It has stopped me in my tracks. It has affected so many of my people in hard ways. It has taken me on a roller coaster ride of my life. Some of you know exactly what I am talking about because you have your story too.

Will we see our circumstances as difficult interruptions or divine interventions? Surrendering our circumstances to God results in a peaceful journey. We are guaranteed a myriad of great adventures in this life. To walk, wander, wonder, or run them with peace is the key to the abundant life. I want this for you on your journey too.

So what was the purpose in me letting you into my story? I said in the beginning it was not just for me but for us. We are told in God's Word to throw off all those things that hinder us and tangle us up, and to look ahead and keep our eyes on the prize at the end of this life. I know my time is on God's side, and so is yours.

I feel God's joy each morning because he said it will be here for me, and I believe it. Do you feel it and believe it too? I know this life is about persevering and enduring through the assignments we are given each day. This gives us opportunity to be launched into the great adventure with God. Peace and joy in the journey are our lifesaving, life-giving power and strength from Jesus. I have humbly learned that I am limited, and God is not. He fills in the blanks if we let him. I learned surrender is a daily thing which gives us freedom to live in peace each and every day.

I experienced the profound truth that God has the plan, and he knows what he is doing. I watched the hand of God working through my trauma, my complications, my joys, my every emotion and circumstance. This story is about gut-wrenching perseverance and endurance. I have learned that I could never dig deep enough to walk through this journey on my own. Jesus did it for me and with me. And he will do it again. I learned we are never alone when we realize who is there with us. When we surrender to God taking the wheel of our lives on this winding road, we are just the passengers along for the ride of our lives.

This story for me was about believing in God's Word and declaring it in the darkness.

This story is about relationships—all of them, you and I have. Your true friends will arrive in your hard places. Embrace them and love them deeply. The ones that couldn't stay, let them go with grace and love them too. Family is very tender in trying times. Hold them close and love them deeply.

This story is God's story through me. It's my Jesus. I would not have gone through this as I have without his hand, his voice, his touch, his teaching, his loving arms there at every moment. Maybe you are on a journey right now that is hard. If you are, this is your time.

Maybe it's COVID; maybe it's something else. We all have a story. I want for you to have a peace that passes all your own understanding wherever you are on your journey.

Dark valleys are dark. Mountains tops are magnificent. Being stuck in the unknown is heavy and hard. But there is peace in each place if we surrender to it.

True peace is not the absence of conflict; true peace is the absence of conflict within in spite of our circumstance.

You might be thinking, *How does one get to this place of surrendered peace?* It requires trusting and believing. That's all, and that is enough. Jesus did it all for us. He continues to do it all; we just need to believe, trust, and walk with him by his spirit (John 3:16).

I had a lot of time on my hands during my COVID adventures. I spent a lot of time using my mind and resting my mind. I spent a lot of time at home, taking time to be still. These months have been my refuge. There is freedom in the quiet. The Lord spoke to me so often during this time of healing. He spoke to me, into me, and through me. Lots of coffee consumed, and a little wine too. Sunshine to take in, thunderstorms to be amazed by, diamonds falling from the sky in the form of snow, and puppies keeping my feet warm. It's been a sweet retreat with my Jesus.

When the Lord spoke to me these past years, I wrote his words down so I would never forget. I think you need to hear them too. The many messages he sent to me to encourage me, to discipline me, to comfort me, to mold and shape me, and to love me so deeply, I believe he sent for me to pay them forward.

I am a better human being today because of these trials. I have learned to love in a way I never thought possible. I love whom I have become in the hard. I want this transformation for you too.

Each adventure with God brings its own story, and he will always be the author of that story.

For you, my friend, I want peace.

40 Days of Divine Devotions

Day 1

In all things

Rejoice always, pray without ceasing, in everything give thanks; for this is the will of God in Christ Jesus for you. (1 Thessalonians 5:16–18 NKJV)

Rejoice in the Lord always. Again, I will say Rejoice! (Philippians 4:4)

I love these verses. Great verses. We read them, we sigh, and we move on. Have we ever really read them and realized what responsibility we have in them?

I think we realize the responsibility, but our obedience and follow-through can be a great weakness.

Let's unpack the richness of these words from scripture.

"Rejoice! Yes, yes, and yes. Rejoice!" Always? Not so much. Our first issue rests there.

Notice in the Philippians verse, it says, "I say it again, 'Rejoice.'" That wasn't by chance. The Lord knows we need reminders because of our being prone to wander. This is a reality for all of us.

The verse goes on to say, "Pray continually." I believe we pray, but continually? Something to ponder.

"Give thanks!" Yes, and amen. We have so many reasons to give thanks! "In all circumstances..." This causes pause, and we can get stuck here. Give thanks in all circumstances? This is not for sissies. It's a challenge that requires help.

"For this is God's will." This just took all options off the table. We don't like this piercing poke of conviction. God's will, not our way.

I think we take God's Word seriously. Our intentions are genuine, but we struggle to live it out seriously. The struggle is real. Why is this? Why don't we? We could list a lot of reasons. I know I have a list. I think you have your own.

The bottom line: We struggle to fully *trust and believe.*

What causes us to not trust? Perhaps we can't grasp that God is who he says he is.

Our emotional state of mind drives us in the wrong direction. We often drive ourselves away from God's truth and get stuck reeling in our emotions. God's Word; it's the constant and consistent go-to for the believer. It's our pathway to protection, promise, provision, and one day perfection. We have to believe this.

What about believing? We often don't run to where we can trust because instead we believe in our own feeble fixes. In those deep-and-hard places, we too quickly jump on the human fast track to nowhere that is filled with chaos and confusion.

And round and round we go. We trust our will and way to be true. It's a human hardship we all face.

We will rejoice always when we trust and believe. It's a choice. When we can, we feel the joy of the Lord rise up within us during those mountaintop experiences. In those hard times, peace covers us like a warm blanket.

Have you experienced this? I have numerous times. What is so amazing and powerful about this is, it goes so against what we expect. When we experience something tragic or extremely difficult, there will be this awkward peace that fills our heart and mind. It's a sweet numbing that carries us through the trial. It is so far beyond us. We couldn't cultivate this calm in the chaos no matter what we could do on our own. Have you been in this surrendered surreal place that is stunningly very real? If you have, you never want to leave.

This is when God becomes very real, and we immediately trust and believe. This is the pathway to experiencing God. Experiencing is believing. When we can believe, we can trust without question. This is faith in action. We rest in the joy of the Lord here in this place. We are in the presence of God doing in us what only God can do.

How do we get to this place of trusting and believing? It's called holy training.

We continue to cultivate our personal relationship with the Lord. We stay steadfast in God's Word where we see the attributes of God. We find everything we need there.

When this discipline becomes consistent and our prayer life becomes constant, we are posturing ourselves in an environment where trusting and believing by faith becomes a natural part of our lives.

Rejoice always, pray without ceasing, and give thanks in all things.

When the storm comes (and it will), when we are in the deep (and we will be), let's choose to trust and believe.

Let's ask for that place of peace we won't want to leave. If we trust and believe, it will be there waiting to carry us through the difficult!

In this world, we will have trouble. Count on it, and count it as joy. Because we have the joy of the Lord and his peace that passes all understanding.

In Christ Jesus, amen.

Day 2

Rainy Days

Let your light so shine before men, that they may see your good works and glorify your Father in heaven. (Matthew 5:16)

A cloudy day can put us in a funk. Some days we don't wake up excited about anything. We feel blah. Some days my coffee isn't tasty or hot enough; my dogs, frankly, are annoying; and my joints and head hurt. I feel fat and ugly, and my mind feels messy too. So how's that for a good morning to you all?

Please tell me you have had these days too.

I used the word *feels* a lot. This word gets us into trouble. Our feelings are the enemy's hook line. He wants to attack us in our feelings. Watch and see for yourself because it is true *every time*.

As soon as we get big feelings, or sense our feeling(s) are on high alert, that's our cue to interrupt these feelings with truth.

Is what I am feeling real? (It might be.)

Is what I am feeling helpful or hopeful?

Is what I am feeling…true? There it is. Is it true?

Nine out of ten times, our circumstance is real, but our feelings are exaggerated.

This is a trick the enemy uses every day, trying to get us to believe the lies he spews. He uses our feelings to distract us. It's a powerful tool that too often works.

How about we remind the enemy about the light in the darkness.

And the light shines in the darkness, and the darkness did not comprehend it. (John 1:5)

We have the power in us because of the light within us to interrupt the enemy's destructive plan with truth *every time*.

So how are you feeling today?

Is it real?

Is it helpful and hopeful?

Is it true?

Ask yourself these questions when your circumstance has put your emotions on high alert.

I may have valid reason to feel this way, but I am the master of my feelings and need to keep them in check. The light shines through the darkness, and we get to choose to bring it each day.

I will choose joy over my feelings. For joy comes in the morning. God says so, and he doesn't lie. When we don't feel his joy, we know who is at work.

Interrupting what we feel with truth and light is the answer to the hard days. We must open up God's Word and fight our feelings with the truth.

On those hard rainy days, let us choose to let our light shine for others to see the love of Christ in us.

Joy comes in the morning even on those rainy days.

Day 3

Those Days

Sometimes we wake up feeling rested, renewed, and ready to face the day before us. Our plans for the day are brought to mind, and we are eager to be about them. We might sing in the shower as we look forward to that hot cup of energy to help capture the day.

Sometimes that isn't the way our feet hit the ground. There are days when before we hit the floor, we are not feeling revived or renewed. This struggle is very real. We drag ourselves out of bed and head to the couch for a couple more minutes of rest or to the coffee pot for that magical fix to our sluggish mood.

We have these good and hard mornings for many reasons. I have my list. Recently it's been an intense jolting combination of both. An intense gratefulness to be alive and resting in that surreal, beautiful place that brings a supernatural energy to *be* present.

Then that other intense reality of how someone put it so well. "That day when I got sick but didn't know I would never feel well or right again." That is some real stuff right there, real hard stuff. That can make finding that promised joy in the morning a very hard find.

But joy is there, and very real too. God is the daily way maker. He is working even if we don't feel it. Let's believe it!

> *But seek first his kingdom and his righteous-*
> *ness, and all these things will be given to you as well.*
> (Matthew 6:33)

This verse is action-packed. We must "seek"; that means set out to do something. That something is to seek *first*, is Christ and his righteousness, even so and no matter what.

When we seek him first, his presence and his Word distracts, redirects, and soothes the hard places we find ourselves in.

When we can see all circumstances from the mind of Christ, we will be content. Easy? Heck no, but being content means freedom. So let's fight that right fight.

> *Not that I speak in regard to need, for I have*
> *learned in whatever state I am, to be content…*
> (Philippians 4:11)

There is a whole other very real aspect to waking up on the wrong side of the bed. I don't think we give this real threat enough attention. When we are not on our A game, this leaves room for a very real enemy to circle us. Have you ever actually felt this? I have.

The devil can't read our mind, but he surely can and will put thoughts in our minds to tangle us up. The enemy brings his game to every opportunity he can. He only has one focus. He longs to distract us. When he can do this, we face a stronghold. His distraction leads to disillusionment, to discouragement, and to disconnection so he can deliver his biggest punch: defeat! Have you been there? I have. I believe we have all fallen into this snare. The enemy is tricky, always prowling around and ready to pounce!

> *The thief does not come except to steal, and to*
> *kill, and to destroy. I have come that they may have*
> *life, and that they may have it more abundantly.*
> (John 10:10)

But…

> *No temptation has overtaken you except such*
> *as is common to man; but God is faithful, who will*
> *not allow you to be tempted beyond what you are*

able, but with the temptation will also make the way of escape, that you may be able to bear it. (1 Corinthians 10:13)

So...

Be sober-minded; be watchful. Your adversary the devil prowls around like a roaring lion, seeking someone to devour. (1 Peter 5:8)

Like 1 Peter says, we are to be sober-minded and watchful. These are not just words. They mean everything for us, not only on those sluggish and cranky days but every day.

The devil isn't just a red pitchfork character part of a story. He is real with the fixated motivation to change the direction in which we are walking. We have the power in us to stand in his way and declare his antics weak and a waste of time in the name of Jesus.

It's the awareness of his reality that must be part of our living out each day.

We have been given the authority to bind and loose. A follower of Christ must know how to operate in authority. Our power source is the Holy Spirit. We've been given this authority to demolish strongholds by the power of the Holy Spirit in us and the mighty Word of God. Our sword!

Our power can be found in God's Word for us. Let's learn to speak. Let's learn to claim the truth!

No weapon formed against you shall prosper, and every tongue which rises against you in judgment, you shall condemn. This is the heritage of the servants of the LORD, and their righteousness is from Me. (Isaiah 54:17)

What if we spoke that over ourselves before our feet hit the ground?

> *You are of God, little children, and have over-*
> *come them, because He who is in you is greater than*
> *he who is in the world.* (1 John 4:4)

So, devil, take that!

And that is just a taste of what we have been given to stand with the name of Jesus over darkness that presses against us.

> *For the LORD your God is He who goes with*
> *you, to fight for you against your enemies, to save*
> *you.* (Deuteronomy 20:4)

So while we will continue to have those days, those hard days and maybe even difficult seasons, let's stand on the promises of God's Word and use the power and authority we have been given!

Be encouraged today, friend.

Day 4

For we are His workmanship, created in Christ Jesus for good works, which God prepared beforehand that we should walk in them. (Ephesians 2:10)

This is a common and often sought out Bible verse for the believer. We are his workmanship. We are called to not work *for* our salvation in this life but to work *out* our salvation. This is very important when it comes to a relationship with Jesus. If you are a Christian working, being, and doing good in hopes that God will find favor in you, then you need to rethink the Gospel in you.

In a relationship with God, we should have an urgent desire to work out the gift of salvation we've been given. Walking through this life is about what Jesus did for us. What we do is his good works provided and presented to us. This is walking *in* the Spirit to work *out* our gift of salvation.

This is a defining day when we get this and desire what's around the next corner with Christ for the Glory of God our Father. It's the great adventure!

Let's stop frantically searching for God's will. Let's start frantically searching for God himself.

The last part of the verse above says: "…which God has prepared beforehand." God's will for us is set up ahead and marked out on the path for us. I believe we can get stuck chasing after the will of God.

"I long to know the will of God for my life."

"We need to choose God's will over our own."

"God's will is better than my way."

We get hung up on God's will when really we should be hung up on God first if we want to know his will.

His will has already been determined, and we have nothing to do with that other than being a follower of him whose will is the best way and better than anything we could offer to the plan.

We chase after God's will because we want to know what it is. We want to know what to do next. We want to plan and prepare so we can serve him well. All good, great, and right stuff with stellar intentions, but what if we committed to a different process?

- What if we would trust that he will bear the responsibility to show us what he wants us to do and how he wants us to do it?
- What if we postured and positioned ourselves in a place to be still, for we know that he will speak through the Holy Spirit to us?
- What if our part was to be still and listen instead of frantically fretting over wanting his will, that our focus would be on him alone?
- What if in the waiting on his will and we were in his Word like a student preparing for their exam, studying his Word teaches us about him so that when he speaks, we can hear and know his voice?
- What if we would realign ourselves to his perspective and refocus ourselves to his purpose? His ways are not our ways. His perspective can be found in his Word. We will never understand his purpose if we don't posture and position ourselves in a place where we can hear and discern his voice.

If we want to know God's will over our ways, we have to change our ways. If we want to know God's will for us, we have to know him and study his ways. If we want to know God's will, we need to be like the sheep who know his voice because that is where we will know what his next best thing is for us.

God's will is God's will. He will reveal it through his Word and as he speaks by the power of the Holy Spirit in us.

How about we do our part to know and experience him, and we allow him to do his part? This is the will of God. When he is found and heard in us, it is then we will be set on solid ground, a firm foundation, ready to do his will.

All Scripture is given by inspiration of God, and is profitable for doctrine, for reproof, for correction, for instruction in righteousness, that the man of God may be complete, thoroughly equipped for every good work. (2 Timothy 3:16–17)

Show me Your ways, O LORD; teach me Your paths. (Psalm 25:4)

In all your ways acknowledge Him, and He shall direct your paths. (Proverbs 3:6)

But the Helper, the Holy Spirit, whom the Father will send in My name, He will teach you all things and bring to your remembrance all things that I said to you. (John 14:26)

My sheep hear My voice, and I know them, and they follow Me. (John 10:27)

Day 5

What's in a Name?

Chapter 1 in the Book of Matthew is about a list of names, the genealogy of Jesus. It's so easy to read right over those long lists, sometimes pages, of names. I got stuck for a minute just on the names, many that I can't even pronounce. Names often come with a means to purpose and power.

One thing I regret never asking my mom before she died was, "Why did you name me Linda?" I think it's a strange-sounding name to my ear. I always have. Every name has a meaning: *Linda* in Spanish means "beautiful." The name *Linda*, "soft, tender," ultimately comes from a Celtic root. Linda isn't found in the Bible, but some connect the name Linda to "serpent." Now that's encouraging! Take some time today to look up the meaning and origin of your name.

If you have kids, why did you choose the names you chose? I think there could be some funny stories with this question. Feel free to use this as a great conversation starter. Maybe a football star, your favorite movie star, or music maker. Some people name their children with a more sentimental motive, such as a grandparent or parent. Names tend to trend. How many babies are given the name Linda today? Every Linda I know is my age! Old names come back like clothing.

When we think about the Bible, names were taken very seriously because their meaning mattered. Names were important, really important. Biblical names are rich in symbolism. Some names signify origin. For example: the very first Book of the Bible, Genesis, itself means "origin." Makes perfect sense. God named the first human Adam, which has likely come from the Hebrew word *ground*.

Makes perfect sense. Then comes Eve, and her name means "living." The mother of all the living.

Makes perfect sense coming from a perfect God.

In the Bible, names can come with a purpose too. Simon is a good example. The name *Simon* means "that hears or obeys." Simon became one of the first to hear God's call to become his disciple. When Jesus called Simon, he got a new name. Peter was his name that Jesus gave him, meaning "rock." On that "rock," Jesus would build his church.

Biblical names can depict a person's traits environment. When God told a hundred-year-old Abraham that his ninety-year-old Sarah would have a son, she laughed. (I might have cried.) God does what he says, so Isaac was born, which means "laughter." I would say very fitting.

Then there is Jesus himself. His name is steeped in symbolism. The name *Jesus* means "savior" and "deliverer." When Mary conceived Jesus through the Holy Spirit, an angel appeared to Joseph in a dream and told Joseph to raise the child as his own and name him Jesus because he will save his people from their sins (Matthew 1:18–21).

There is said to be 198 different names for God, but actually many more when we start reading his long list throughout the Word of God.

Why so many names for the King? The Bible was written to reveal God to us. We get to know God by His Living Word. We see his character, nature, and his purpose and plan through the many names he reveals to us. We read about God to teach us his ways and what he has done, is doing, and continues to do throughout history.

Here are just a few:

- Elohim (God)
- Yahweh (Lord, Jehovah)
- El Elyon (The Most High God)

- Adonai (Lord, Master)
- El Shaddai (Lord God Almighty)
- El Olam (The Everlasting God)
- Jehovah Jireh (The Lord Will Provide)
- Jehovah Rapha (The Lord Who Heals You)
- Jehovah Nissi (The Lord Is My Banner)
- El Qanna (Jealous God)
- Jehovah Mekoddishkem (The Lord Who Sanctifies You)
- Jehovah Shalom (The Lord Is Peace)
- Jehovah Sabaoth (The Lord of Hosts)
- Jehovah Raah (The Lord Is My Shepherd)
- Jehovah Tsidkenu (The Lord Our Righteousness)
- Jehovah Shammah (The Lord Is There)

This name doesn't only have symbolism but carries a huge responsibility. His name means everything for us. His name is the name above all names. There is only one God who holds the whole world in his hand. His name matters!

There is a lot to consider in a name!

> *Therefore God also has highly exalted Him and given Him the name which is above every name, that at the name of Jesus every knee should bow, of those in heaven, and of those on earth, and of those under the earth, and that every tongue should confess that Jesus Christ is Lord, to the glory of God the Father.* (Philippians 2:9–11)

Day 6

Now Is the Acceptable Time

*But sanctify the Lord God in your hearts, and always be
ready to give a defense to everyone who asks you a reason
for the hope that is in you, with meekness and fear;*
—1 Peter 3:15

I had the night shift at the homeless shelter. A crazy night it was.
Everyone has story, a situation, and circumstance filled with victories
and with pain. I am reminded it's a pretty small world after all and
that everyone matters.

I waited to write until everyone was sleeping. I started and
stopped writing numerous times because people were weary and restless. They had burdens and real-life stuff they were wrestling with.
God is concerned about the homeless hearts too. I felt honored to
being available to listen.

"Now is the acceptable time" are five captivating words. *Now*,
as in right now, could be daunting. *Acceptable* is a tricky word. Who
decides? And *time* is a word that reminds me that we never have
enough.

However, no matter how we read those five words, one of this
is certain. God's timing is perfect *no matter where we are*. When he
speaks to us, and he does, we need to respond with obedience. Yes,
Lord. When God announces that now is the acceptable time, what
we do is critical. When we run into that stranger who has a question,

are we prepared to offer the love of Jesus? Are we prepared to meet them where they are at or tackle an unexpected need?

Do we meet them with a look, a smile, and with our time to spend the time they need? What about when we are with our kids? Are we ready in and out of season to be Christlike so that no matter the trial, they see Jesus in us? When we are with friends, when we are at work or with family—wherever we find ourselves each and every day, *now is the time.*

It comes down to this: we will obey or disobey. It's either faith or unbelief. Obedience or disobedience. There is nothing in between because God's timing is always perfect, and he is never late. He is asking us to join him where he is already at work. Will we trust him in the awkward? We will trust him outside our comfort zone? We will trust him as we go into uncomfortable places? Will we simply say, "Yes, Lord"? He wants us to share his love and message with the world, and *now* is the acceptable time!

When we decide to follow Jesus until the end, we decide that we will go frightened into the unchartered places and spaces only to find that God's Holy Spirit knows just what to do and what to say when we don't. We can leave fear at the door and walk in the Spirit of God by faith because God knows in advance the path we will take if we will choose to trust and obey.

As we look around our little corners of this big world, we see trouble and uncertainty for sure all around us. It's a new day today, and we get to choose how we will navigate. We each have a different journey that we are on. It's personal and uniquely individual. But for each of us, God extends his invitation knowing that his resources are more than adequate for any assignment he gives us.

It's truly the great adventure, and *now* is the acceptable time!

Day 7

Come...It's a Divine Invitation

Come to me with humility in your heart, bowing before my infinite Intelligence. Relinquish your demand to understand; accept the fact that many things are simply beyond your comprehension.

Why? Because I am infinite, and you are finite.

In layman's term: He is God, and we are not.

This goes against what the voices of today are shouting or quietly distracting us with.

Let's unpack this powerful message.

"Come to me with humility in your heart."

It doesn't say, "Think about me"; it says, "Come to me," which means "a commitment to go forth." We are to bring our mind and soul to Christ.

"With humility in our heart."

We don't just come willy-nilly or all puffed up to Christ. We come with a heart of humility. That doesn't just happen. Our human flesh fights against this. We must give up to self and dig deep to reach a place of humility. Jesus is saying, "Come to me after you surrender our mind, attitudes, and pride." He wants us raw so we can be ready to receive what he has for us. Not a simple request.

Next: "Bowing before my infinite intelligence."

We can see now why we are to come humbly! To *bow down* means "to show intentional weakness by agreeing to the demands or following the orders of someone or something." Our flesh will wrestle with this posture every time. Jesus says, "Humbly come, and he knows our hearts." If we don't empty ourselves, chances are, we won't stay.

We are asked to bow to an intelligence we will never fully grasp. This seems utterly crazy to bow to someone we can't even get our heads wrapped around. We don't by nature live like this. We want to be in the know and fully in control. We like our questions answered and to understand our next move. This is how we operate. Will we obey anyway?

Next: "Relinquish your demand to understand. Accept the fact that many things are simply beyond your comprehension."

We are asked to give up our demanding attitude to understand. This right here can be the deal breaker. We, in our human flesh, are bent to walk away, or will we decide to walk his way? With God, there is no middle road. We accept or reject.

It then says, "We need to accept the fact, the truth, that there are many things in God's economy that we can't comprehend!" This drips with surrender. Being willing to surrender our will, our way, and our need to have access to the unknown, to the unseen that promises us beyond the world. It's risky!

This is where we can find our human self wrestle with why because simply (but not so simply) God is God, and we are not. We get to decide to trust and believe or not. Accept or reject.

There is only one thing that will allow us to release our grip: *faith*. It's a complicated word that will transform us to a place we never want to leave but requires us to leave ourselves behind and go by faith. Faith is the basic and key ingredient to begin a relationship with God.

To release our grip means we choose to believe and rest in things beyond our understanding.

Choosing to believe in something and someone far bigger than our brain can consume is surrender. This is faith in a king. His name is Jesus.

People will think we are crazy. Count on this. We will be dismissed because the world doesn't give his peace a chance. We may be forced to walk alone but will never be lonely. It's a risk worth taking.

The believer, follower of Jesus, will humbly bow to the one, the only one, who was born then died for you and for me to have eternal life. That would be enough, but after three days, he rose again. No one, not one, can claim this. Jesus is set apart from all other four thousand religions in the world! I want to be on his team.

> *For God so loved the world that He gave His only begotten Son, that whoever believes in Him should not perish but have everlasting life.* (John 3:16)

His Words are filled with promises that the world could never offer. Never. Nada.

Will you come, humbly willing to trust and believe what you can't see?

I did, and it had wreaked me in the most mind-blowing heart settling way! There are no words to describe this love, and it's okay. I don't need to fully understand the details of this divine dance, and it's okay. I can walk into unchartered territory unafraid and unaffected by the wilds of this world, and it's okay.

Why, because I am loved by a King that will never leave me nor forsake me. I will walk right into forever one day. That day will be a glorious day.

Who would not want to come?

> *Come to me with humility in your heart, bowing before my infinite Intelligence. Relinquish your demand to understand; accept the fact that many things are simply beyond your comprehension.* (Sarah Young, *Jesus Calling: Embracing Joy in His Presence* [2016], 65)

Then He said to them all, "If anyone desires to come after Me, let him deny himself, and take up his cross daily, and follow Me." (Luke 9:23)

Will you come?

Day 8

Living in the Light

What is the evidence that you are, or I am, living in the light?

Living in the light means having surrendered our life to living under the authority and with the power of Jesus Christ *in* us. It means living this life on purpose to bringing light into the darkness. It means wading through the muddy waters with discernment. It means being sensitive to the down and dirty, and taking our duty very seriously for such a time as this. Really, it means everything.

Take some time today and read this amazing scripture: 1 Thessalonians 5:1–11.

We have evidence of a renewed character.

Those who live in the light possess a radically different nature. We are not content to remain in sin. Repentance is part of our ongoing process along with confession and forgiveness.

This process heightens our awareness of sin and makes us sensitive to the conviction of the Holy Spirit. Paul calls this being in a state of being watchful and sober. "Conviction" doesn't feel good, but it's so very good for us. It's the Holy Spirit in us guiding our will onto the path of God's way. It's pulling us from the edge when we get too close. It's reminding us of who we are in the light.

When we are living in a state of moral and spiritual watchfulness, we have a renewed character.

The evidence of radical conduct:

The Christian way of life is radical conduct by the world's stan-dards. They don't know what to do with us. They don't know how it's possible to hate sin but still truly and genuinely love the sinner and love this life with them. We know, as a follower of Jesus, that convic-tion is for the sinner to wrestle with, and our job is to love them apart from their sin. We are to catch them when they fall.

Why does this make perfect sense to the follower? Because as a believer living in the forgiveness of sins, we have experienced first-hand the process of our sinful nature moving to conviction in order to experience the freedom in forgiveness that only Christ can give.

Jesus paid a huge price to pour out this love upon us. So we love the sinner; we love the enemy because we understand that freedom for them is just one surrendered decision away. We want our hearts to break for what breaks the heart of Christ.

This goes against the world's agenda, yet we know that light shines in the darkness so we know that that love is not an option.

The evidence of reliable compensation:

As we look around today more than ever, we can see that the world is going insane right before our eyes. Our government is fail-ing us, and our nation is hopelessly divided. This secular agenda is tearing our culture down. Where moral absolutes were once compro-mised, today we live in an anti-moral environment. Hard to hear, but it's true. This is the way of the world. However, the way of the master is still alive. We must never lose sight of this truth.

The follower of Christ must keep their eyes fixed on the prom-ises of God in the midst of the world's agenda. A great reward awaits those who place their faith in Christ alone. This is the target we fixate on. Our reward is sure; our compensation is reliable.

The physical condition of the body doesn't matter for the fol-lower. What matters as we take this closer walk toward eternity? It's our spiritual condition and conduct that matters.

We need to be encouraging one another, spurring each other toward the goal to reach the prize. We must throw off those things that hinder and trip us up.

We should not be sitting around waiting for God's next move. We are too be busy about hating the sin but loving the sinner because our character is being cultivated to the character of Christ. We have been created for this. Let's finish well as we bring light into the darkness.

We won't fix the troubles of today; it's not our role or job. Jesus is coming, and he is in charge of making all things new. Let's not fight the wrong fight, but instead let's live with purpose in a posture of intentionally loving others like Jesus does. This will no doubt keep us busy until we meet Jesus face to face.

Do you have a bright light to share?

Love wins.

Day 9

A Small Thing

So Jesus said to them, "Because of your unbelief; for assuredly, I say to you, if you have faith as a mustard seed, you will say to this mountain, 'Move from here to there,' and it will move; and nothing will be impossible for you." (Matthew 17:20)

If you are a follower of Christ, you've heard this verse and probably referred to it on occasion. But what does it really mean? I have gotten a bit fixated on this mustard seed thing.

So what does faith like a mustard seed even mean?

A big mistake that is often made is to think that power is sourced in faith itself. The mustard seed and faith are connected in the Bible, but we want to unpack its purpose and path correctly. Why does Jesus use a mustard seed to describe faith? That's a good question. Jesus uses many things, sometimes odd things in the Bible to teach us important things. A mustard seed...kind of an odd object for sure. In Jesus's day, the mustard seed was used proverbially to represent the smallest of things. And with a diameter of one to two millimeters, it's a fitting illustration.

When we hear the big word faith, we go there, we seek it, we fear it, we find it, and our desire and goal is to grow it strong. Faith, a very big and important word for the follower lined up with a little tiny seed. Seems strange, doesn't it?

By using this tiny seed to describe faith, Jesus is directing our attention not to the quantity or strength of our faith but to the *object* of our faith. Our faith is only as strong as the object in which it's placed. I had to read that a couple of times because I so often I have placed my focus on and get fixated on faith, the weakness of it with a desire to have a strong faith so that I could be content. Strong faith equals strong Christian? Isn't that the goal? Does anyone else have a mind that goes there?

It's true that a strong faith is to be grown and cultivated. Faith is the foundation to our journey. This is important. But when faith is connected to this little seed, it is speaking to us about the object of our faith, not faith itself. If our faith, even if it's the size of a mustard seed, is placed in the all-powerful God, great things can happen. It is not necessary to have great big strong faith; even a small faith is enough as long as it is faith in the one and only great God. God is the object of our faith, and he is a big God. He can get great things done with our little faith.

The Bible defines faith as a self-emptied, dependent assurance in God's character and promises. I love this! The most famous biblical definition of faith is Hebrews 11:1 which says, "*Now faith is the substance of things hoped for, the evidence of things not seen.*"

The content of that faith is clarified in Hebrews 11 verse 6: "*But without faith it is impossible to please Him, for he who comes to God must believe that He is, and that He is a rewarder of those who diligently seek Him.*"

Biblical faith has nothing to do with personal self-effort (Ephesians 2:8–9) and has no reliance on human strength and wisdom (1 Corinthians 2:5). In other words, when we talk about biblical faith, all the strength and power come from the object of faith (God himself), not the size of faith—even a mustard seed faith will do. Doesn't this cause you to sigh? It did me. It gives me permission to be a work in progress and still cared for.

It always comes down to God first in all things for all things!

Do we believe with our little faith that God will move that mountain? If we do believe this, God will do great things his way and by his timing with his plan and for his purpose. By faith, we must believe.

Have you experienced big things happening in your life with your small faith? I have many times. God is so faithful and makes things happen when I am aware and unaware too.

It's not the amount of faith which brings the impossible within reach but the power of God, which is available to even the smallest faith. I think we can so easily misplace our faith too. I wonder if we want to attach our control to our faith instead of standing on the promises of God, believing by faith, if even just a little?

It's also important to not dismiss our "Oh, me of little faith" as okay. The longer we walk in the Spirit of God, the more our desire and urgency to cultivate and grow our faith never ends. This is a very important work in process for progress in each of us. Let's not miss this and settle for our little faith.

The point of this little mustard seed is that God can do big, bold, and amazing things even as we fall short with a weak and small faith.

God can do the impossible. He is the object of our faith. I can't help but believe if we really understand this and settle this faith thing with God, our faith will puff up with a mighty strength as we walk in a spirit of believing.

Be blessed and encouraged, friend.

Day 10

This, Too, Shall Pass

Did you ever just have one of those seasons? One of those times in life where you just can't catch a break. Where one thing after another causes unexpected pauses that don't feel good. When you feel you are taking three steps back and losing traction with every decision or lack of. Yeah, me too.

It's been a bumpy road in our home for a number of months. Lots of surprises on this crazy adventure called life. Some that simply have no words, and others that have set us back too.

Life begins to look differently when you are taken on roads you've not planned nor seen before. My motto for many years has been "This, too, shall pass." Those "this's" do pass and hopefully leave us a little braver and way stronger than when we met them. These bumps are like taking one's faith to the gym for a workout too. Always an adventure. Easy? So not easy, but so very grateful for a good, good Father who is always there to help us along the way.

We had been so excited to welcome a dear friend from the Dominican Republic. Anticipating this day brought an element of anxious excitement. He arrived on a Saturday with a hug that was long overdue. This guy is far beyond his years. He showed up in a big way—long distance—these past months when the valley was very deep and real for me. Having his visit is a big breath of fresh air. I needed to see him face-to-face and experience Wilson in this time of my life. Is there someone in your life that when they are present, you just feel safe? It's hard to explain, but it's a really good place to be.

We had plans. We were going to do the many American things he liked to do. It was exciting to think about. And then he had a little cough. With the excitement of Easter coming, knowing our whole family would be together, his cough warranted a well-known nose invasion! The COVID test.

And then yes, he was positive. We thanked the Lord that his case was mild. He was sick but not struggling much at all. We were so grateful for this. Our fun plans quickly ran into the proverbial brick wall. He was locked away in our home, and bleach became the new air freshener. Meals were set by his door, and texting from room-to-room was our communication. A flat-screen propped on his dresser helped pass the time a bit.

The days were filled with changing airline tickets and talking to the health department to figure out the rules. It felt surreal. If I were a swearing girl, there would be a blue streak. I felt so disappointed, disturbed, and sad having to lock our friend away. For our safety, it was necessary, but it didn't feel good at all.

But then I stop to think about the blessings all around me, and even though the past year or so had been hard, I realized I was still so grateful for each day, no matter what may come. As I sat in the quiet one night, texting my friend between walls, I asked the Lord if he could slow the hard just a tad. I was beginning to feel the weight of the seemingly long-term burden yet filled with his peace, even in this new mess we were in.

Our dear friend spent his entire stay in his jail. (Felt that way.) We decided that instead of mourning the loss of our well-intended plans, we would begin again. We started planning another trip where we could be together. Those feelings of anticipation arose again. We hugged that big hug I so longed for on his way to the security in the airport. We were both excited about our next well-made plans to be.

I learned in that hard brief season that no matter how things play out, don't stop dancing, and don't stop planning because "this, too, shall pass." Always be in anticipation for the next great adventure. What a difference it makes when we posture ourselves with an attitude of gratitude even in the hard seasons. When in the hard, we remind ourselves that yes, "this too shall pass"; our angst and anxiety are washed away.

> *And the peace of God, which surpasses all understanding, will guard your hearts and minds through Christ Jesus.* (Philippians 4:7)

With the peace of Christ within, there is nothing that can overtake us because he has overcome. This life comes with burdens, bad times, bruises, and unexpected interruptions but also too many blessings to count. Little and big, they are there for us. Let's not miss them in the midst of the hard season.

If you have found yourself in a valley with crazy things around every corner, tighten your seatbelt and anticipate the blessed moments Jesus has for you along the way.

> *Peace I leave with you, my peace I give to you; not as the world gives do I give to you. Let not your heart be troubled, neither let it be afraid.* (John 14:27)

So whatever may come to pass, we can say: "This, too, shall pass."

Be blessed!

Wilson

Day 11

Wait

Have you ever had to wait? Let me phrase that differently. Have you ever been given the choice to give up your place in line? Has a choice ever been taken from you?

If you say no, the truth is not within you. Sorry, but that's how this life rolls.

Ask ten third-graders to form a straight line. Nine will clamor to be first in line. Every time! They will do this even if they are clueless as to why the lineup.

They all want to be first.

Ask a thirty-, forty-, fifty-, sixty-year-old adult to get in line for a promotion, a chance to win a new car, a vacation, or maybe a cleaning lady once per month, or even a nap without interruption. We can all write our own list. We all want to be first for our own self-made reasons. It's who we are.

We've been trained well by the world we live in. Last one standing gets the leftovers, feels embarrassed, or less than. Been there? I have too. How does it feel? I don't know about you, but when I end up last or don't get what I want or worked really hard for, I can feel mad, cheated, sad, jealous, lonely, betrayed, and even forgotten. Those words have not been imprinted by our creator. So when we find ourselves in this ugly place, we have choices to make. Because we have been given free will, we get to choose how we will react and how we will respond.

We might be quick to say, "I am okay letting others have it all," or "I am okay with bringing up the rear." But seldom and maybe never does our flesh say that. That's where the rubber meets the road because words are cheap and will never fool the one who has our hearts.

Matthew 19:30 is a good place for us to start and to finish.

> *But many who are first will be last, and the last first.* (Matthew 19:30)

The disciples too were accustomed to the common habits of man. Those guys were no different than we are really. They fought for the position too. Note the word *fought*. They were a feisty bunch. Jesus addresses this issue of coming in first because he knew we would struggle in our flesh. According to Christ, "Worthy is the man who has forgotten his superiority and humbles himself."

He has forgotten! I want to erase this challenge from my mind. Are you with me? Christ says, "He declares that they who abase themselves, (meaning consider themselves less) means are the greater." Christ says we should live in a posture where if we lose, in Jesus's culture, we win. We need to learn to live like Jesus did. This is a powerful message for us.

> *Let nothing be done through selfish ambition or conceit, but in lowliness of mind let each esteem others better than himself.* (Philippians 2:3)

Can you see here in this verse where we are called to be set apart? The world cannot accept such a thing. The truth is, we won't make sense to the world. We will look foolish, and by the world's account, they will have placed us last because we don't fit the "me mold." We are taught to be selfless.

If you are a believer, a follower of Christ, we know about that narrow road. We will be pressed hard to humbly walk the talk. If we listen to the world, we will hear, "Greatness consists of how many we lead." Listening to the Lord speaks the very opposite: "Greatness consists of how many we serve."

We can push to the head of the line and receive the world's applause, or we can give up our place in line and hear God's "well done." The servant of God knows his place.

Maybe you needed this message today too. May you be strengthened by the power of Christ in you.

> *Let each of you look out not only for his own interests, but also for the interests of others.* (Philippians 2:4)

> *Let nothing be done through selfish ambition or conceit, but in lowliness of mind let each esteem others better than himself.* (Philippians 2:3)

> *For I say, through the grace given to me, to everyone who is among you, not to think of himself more highly than he ought to think, but to think soberly, as God has dealt to each one a measure of faith.* (Romans 12:3)

> *He must increase, but I must decrease.* (John 3:30)

Day 12

The Great "I Will"

We are all familiar with the Great I AM in Scripture. We get to learn a lot about who God is through his divine statements of the Great I AM.

Did you know there are also "I Will" statements in the New Testament? Thirty of them actually.

When we say "I will," we are saying something with a stamp on it. It sends trust and love with it.

"I will be there." "I will do that." "I will never do that again." "I will make this happen."

What happens when I am not there or I don't do or I do it again or I don't make it happen? That is what too often happens in our human flesh. We fall short with others. We've all done it and experienced the pain both ways. "I will" says "I promise." These words hold a lot of power that affects our hearts greatly. What happens when a promise is broken? We are filled with a many of big feelings. Our emotions can explode; trust can be broken; and relationships, broken. A broken promise can wreak us. This is a big deal.

Why do we put so much risk into a promise?

It is not just empty words out of a person's mouth. A reckless text on the phone. It is not meaningless words on a sheet of paper. A promise is a commitment, and it is meant to be taken seriously. A promise is hard work! It's sacrifice. When we make a promise to someone, it will change our plans; it will almost always interrupt our schedule. We will have to reach farther for someone else. It won't be about us.

A promise has love attached to it. The message of a promise is an affirmation of love, respect, friendship, and human connection. It says, "Someone cares enough about me."

I can't help but think about Jesus when we think about promise. Jesus's promises are so set apart from what the world can offer. To be honest, we ourselves fail too. We fall short on our promises, but Jesus never did and never will. That is power, and we get to be in the receiving end!

What a savior; what a master and friend we have in Jesus.

Let's look at just some of his promises.

Be encouraged as you spend some time meditating on the verses below.

Let's start with our salvation:

I will never drive you out. (John 6:37)

Jesus promises that all whom the Father calls, he will not drive away. He backs up this promise by telling us he will never leave nor forsake us.

He will be with us; he will not leave or forsake us. (Deuteronomy 31:8)

This world could never promise us this.

"I will make you fishers of men." (Matthew 4:19)

He does not say, "Follow me, and I will assign you tasks you think you're knowledgeable of." Christ is clearly promising that if we just follow him, he will do the work in us. He will transform us into disciples who will be used.

I will show you what he is like who comes to me and hears my words and puts them into practice... (Luke 6:47)

Here we find Jesus promising his guidance to understand truth. He will give us guidance to make right decisions in our lives. He will help us understand his will.

Come to me, all who are weary and burdened, and I will *give you rest.* (Matthew 11:28)

This is so powerful! Where would we be without this promise? I know where I would be. A heap on the floor most days! This life is not for sissies, and we need a place to exhale; to really rest; and to find comfort that runs deep and changes the course of our mindset, our mood, and our emotions.

The powerhouse of all promises!

And I will ask the father, and he will give you another counselor to be with you forever. (John 14:16)

Read that again. We get a double "I will" here. What a gift in this promise!

God doesn't miss a thing. Our life here is set up to win if we will accept his way. We are promised to not be left to navigate this world on our own. We have the Holy Spirit in us to guide us, to teach us along the way. We get to decide what kind of student we will be.

And if I go and prepare a place for you, I will come back and take you to be with me that you also may be where I am. (John 14:3)

Most people walk through their earthly life preparing for their futures. People invest money so they may retire comfortably. Parents write wills so that their children are taken care of when they're gone.

We even make weekly plans and lists for the next day's activities. We also know the world can take all our well-thought-out and hard-worked-for plans and wreck them. We have all been here.

But not with Jesus. No, not with Jesus! We get a promise about our future. And it's one that is perfect. One that required a big sacrifice and cost him everything.

Do we understand the love in this promise? We live in a world of brokenness, and in a place where words are cheap and trust is a far reach. We feel most days that it's all falling apart, but in reality, it's all falling right into place. A promise is a big deal.

We are promised the full blessings of God because Jesus said, "I will."

Day 13

What is it all about, anyway?

Have you ever wondered, *What is this all about?* or *What am I here for, anyway?*

Do we get so busy about doing this life that we don't even stop to give purpose a thought? Some of us are raising kids, keeping marriages alive, tending to aging parents, going to school or college, or getting a master's degree in something that really matters. Maybe you are in a season of searching. You might be in a job that has gone nowhere or has taken you everywhere. Where we land is where we tend to identify our purpose in this life.

Our plans or intentions actually have little to do with the real plan. We like to identify where we land because we are in a state of doing. I believe doing walks out our purpose, but that doesn't define our purpose.

When something feels right or is exciting, challenging, or fits our timing or schedule, we call that our purpose. When it's working out, it fits perfectly in our purpose box.

But does it? If you are like me, I knew what I would be career wise since I was about five years old. Maybe you are still asking the question, What will I be when I grow up? or you might be in the lane, "I am never growing up, much less desiring to be anything. I will just take one day at a time." We are all in a state of doing something.

For me, once I was able to identify my purpose in God's story for this life, what I was "doing" was no longer what got me up and going each day. God has shaped and prepared us to play a unique role in each step of his story in our lives. The reason we are here on this Earth is for so much more than living our best life. God wants us to partner with him in helping advance his kingdom in heaven here on earth. He doesn't want us to miss moments with him, experience him, or to see him at work in his glory. What a privilege. It's all for him and about him. When I realized this, my life got exciting, and I finally had solid ground to launch from.

The great adventure begins with us waking up each day with anticipation of how God is going to invite us to go on mission with him. When he gives us our assignment for a day or for a season, we lose sight of what used to be, and we are fixated on his kingdom work. It truly is the great adventure.

We begin to live differently. We see with different eyes. We see the world and people differently too. What becomes most radical is that this life is no longer about us. Once I got this, I became free to be instead of running on the gerbil wheel of doing.

There are still unknowns and challenges along the way, but that is all part of the great adventure of being on purpose with Christ. A friend recently told me she feels she has no purpose. This affects every choice and challenge we meet. It begs that question, what is this life all about, anyway?

It has a profound effect on us. The Bible tells us to ask, to seek, and we shall find.

God is the author of our story!

He will reveal his purpose and invite us to join him where he is already working. He is building this kingdom; he invites us to join him and gives us assignments along the way. This is where the adventure gets a bit crazy—good crazy.

Someone said to me, "So you just wait for God to move you from here to there"? That is a really good question. The answer is tricky because I believe it's a yes and no. No help, right?

God created us with a brain to think, to discern, to plan, and to choose.

We are to use the gifting we have and be busy about planning each day out. That is the doing part of our purpose. But the Bible also says we make a plan, but God directs our path. This is the adventure part. We might have a well-thought-out plan, and *bam*, our plan takes a U-turn or changes up from what we had worked it to be. We have to learn to make our plans with what God has given us but to hold them very loosely at the same time. That is the yes-and-no answer.

We have to remember and believe that God's plan is always perfect and fashioned for our best. We have to be ready and willing to surrender our plan to his plan. So how do we know if it's his plan? His plan usually comes out of nowhere but makes sense. It lines up with his word, and we feel pulled toward it. But if chaos and confusion fill our circumstance or situation, that is a pretty clear sign we have gotten off the path, or the enemy is attempting to invade and destroy what God has for good. This is very opposite of God's nature or design for our days.

Sometimes we will be in the waiting room. The waiting is the hard part because the adventure can appear to be halted. This is when class begins. In the wait, we are to be learning. In the wait, God is preparing and equipping us for the next assignment or to continue where he left off. Let's pray that we would be good students in these challenging waits. If we can be obedient in the wait, we are soon to be back on adventure with our teacher and author, the one writing our story.

Can we ask for his purpose to be revealed in our lives? I think we can.

1. Pray for vision and instruction (Proverbs 29:18).
2. Pray for confidence in the revealed purpose (Jeremiah 29:11).
3. Pray for direction (Proverbs 19:21).
4. Pray for wisdom (James 1:5).
5. Pray for unshakeable faith (1 Thessalonians 5:24).
6. Pray for peace as you live out purpose (Philippians 4:6–7, 9).
7. Pray for trust in God (Proverbs 3:5–6).

Day 14

It wasn't raining

Did you know when God commanded Noah to build the ark, rain was not in the forecast. There had *never* been rain.

Rain wasn't born yet. Ponder that for a minute. If these Bible stories are just silliness and fairy tales for you, enjoy the story. For the follower of Jesus Christ, sit on that for a bit. The idea of rain was unknown, yet Noah built the Ark.

Noah's Ark was not a bathtub! It was a ship built 4,350 years ago: 510 feet long, 85 feet wide, and 51 feet high. Why an ark? Why Noah?

The quick story goes like this: When God created the earth and man, he said it was good until it wasn't. It didn't take long for man to fall away and go their own way. The world at that time was messed up! The Lord saw how utterly wicked the people had become. Every thought was evil, so God said, "I'm done. Enough of this!" He actually said, *"I will destroy from the earth the people I created, and with them the animals, birds and creeping things"* (Genesis 6:5–7).

God's plan feels unkind, but what if things had remained? Sometimes a restart is the only way to redemption. God's plan with Noah was part of the big picture we've been living all along. He is a good, good Father!

Why Noah? Everyone was evil and had lost their minds and God's way.

Why would God choose Noah?

What was different about him?

Genesis 6:8–10 tells us that "Noah found favor with God." Noah was a follower of God, not man. He was a righteous man in the midst of evil all around him. Noah didn't cave into peer pressure. God established a covenant with him. What a righteous risk Noah took to stand out, stand apart, from the world around him. Human stakes were high. Heavenly rewards were going to happen.

Why would God choose Noah? It all comes down to one word: faith.

Noah had what had to be a supernatural faith in God. It couldn't have been of himself. God entrusted this boat assignment to Noah because Noah was righteous and filled with a faith understandable and undeniable.

> Faith sees the invisible, believes the unbe-
> lievable, and receives the impossible. (Corrie Ten
> Boone)

Can we even imagine Noah receiving this command? I don't think so. The world he lived in was bad. Really bad. People were not to be trusted and were wicked evil.

No one had ever seen nor heard of rain, and God says there is going to be a flood! "Build a boat, a really big one, Noah. Do it this way." Rain, flood, boat, what? What would you do? What would I do?

It took 150 days to build the boat. Can you imagine the ridicule from these evil people? Can you imagine how set apart Noah had to feel? One man on an island that soon would disappear 150 days (which translates to a long time). He persevered under great persecution. He didn't give up when he didn't understand. He had to be clueless. Rain? "This is one big boat, God, and I don't even know what a boat is. But I will build this thing, I will follow your way, and I will trust you even so!" Outstanding obedience.

In my comfy little world, when my little boat gets rocked a bit, do I raise my sword and forge forward with unwavering faith? Or do I say, "Oh, this is one of those times I am supposed to have faith, so I guess I need to be digging deep to find it!"? I think the biggest mistake we often make is digging for something that is already there! Do I practice faith enough so that it becomes a part of me, second nature? Do I choose to trust, obey, and walk in what I already have, or constantly go digging for it?

Noah was too busy digging post holes and pounding something to dig for his faith! I believe faith became all he had to hold on to in this uncertainty he was facing. One plank at a time for 150 days.

It came to be this massive wooden thing called a boat. The wicked world around him, I am sure, mocked him, laughed at him, and deemed him a crazy person. Just imagine that scene for a moment. Noah was going against the flow in a big way. But God said, "I am making a new way, and I am using my righteous man, Noah, to do it."

It was Noah, his family, his faith, and his God. Isn't that just the way God says it should be? Evidently, Noah thought so because he never gave in or gave up. It was faith one day at a time.

So the flood. Noah and the people quickly learned about rain. Trouble came with a vengeance. They didn't see it coming, and there it was upon them.

The Bible says the fountains of the deep broke open, and the windows of heaven opened. Rain poured (not sprinkled) for forty days and nights (Genesis 7:17–24).

I am thinking about Noah when the rain came. He had to be thinking, *I like this new and big thing called boat!* When the waters raged and rose, Noah continued to listen for God's voice as he gathered what God instructed him to do, and he sailed away. Noah was an obedient servant! One hundred fifty days to build this boat, and one hundred fifty days to sail in it. Imagine that trip to somewhere. Water raging, stomachs turning, animals everywhere doing their thing. After about forty days, I am sure it had to feel like the wilderness! This surely was not the cruise we think of today. It had to get old and stinky, depressing and dull.

Noah had to be thinking, *When will this end? I have been on a journey I didn't ask for and surely do not understand. And frankly, I am tired and weary!* (Sound familiar?) I can hear Jesus saying to him,

*Come to me, all who labor and are heavy
laden, and I will give you rest.* (Matthew 11:28)

Yet faith in his God was all he had to hang on to. So he did. Unwavering obedience.

He could have given up. He could have jumped ship, but then he would not have experienced redemption—the end of the story. Thank you, Noah!

When that big boat reached land with a big thump, I have to wonder if Noah ran to the heavy-weighted doors to escape, or if he just sat there in his well-lived faith and said, "Uh oh, what's next on this great adventure?" I hope the latter, because what an adventure with his great God it was.

Noah got out and got busy with his next assignment, but before he did, he took time to *worship his king.*

This part of the story should not be overlooked. He made time, taking time to give glory and praise to his God. (I may have just passed out on the beach for a week.)

God's voice spoke a message for all mankind in that moment. "Never again will I curse the ground because of man, or send a flood to destroy all living things even though mankind's heart is evil from childhood."

God blessed Noah that day and said, "Be fruitful and increase in number and fill the earth."

Noah had to be saying, "Thank you, God! No more boat-building!" Or maybe he rejoiced with God in his faithfulness because of God's steadfast faithfulness to him.

The massive takeaway of this amazing story is not the flood or the boat (although mighty amazing); it's the example of faith and how we get to experience the intimate fullness of God when we trust and obey by faith.

Today I can't help but think about our world today and the faith it takes to walk in it. We are in a flood of uncertainty no doubt. We can feel like we are tossed from this to that like a boat in a storm lost at sea. Noah is our guy! And God is our rescue.

Faith is not for the faint. It's a force that releases our fear when we trust and obey it.

Let's walk, work, and worship by faith like Noah.

Let's look at our situations, schedules, and circumstances as a great adventure with God.

Let's remember that our faith forces fear out so we can walk in obedience to experience the abundant life God has provided.

God said he promised he would never wreak the world with a flood again, but he said this:

> And if I go and prepare a place for you, I will come again and receive you to Myself, that where I am, there you may be also. (John 14:3)

> Behold, He is coming with clouds, and every eye will see Him, even they who pierced Him. And all the tribes of the earth will mourn because of Him. Even so, Amen. (Revelation 1:7)

> But concerning that day and hour no one knows, not even the angels of heaven, nor the Son, but the Father only. (Matthew 24:36)

Day 15

Go

I used to be the lady that said, "Give me ten minutes and I will be ready to go anywhere!" It was true and still is today. I have an entire to-go setup ready to go on a moment's notice. I love to travel and experience culture and new surroundings. It's hard to keep this girl down.

Do you have a to-go setup too?

Have you ever been in that good place? That place where you can finally exhale. That place you worked really hard to get to. That place that is comfortable without the struggle finally? Writing this actually feels good. I am feeling pressure lifting somehow. Maybe you know what I am speaking of.

The followers of Christ know that this comfortable place isn't where we belong for long.

Our master commands us to go. We need permission to stay. The world begs us to live in the reverse. We long to stay where it feels good, safe, and comfortable.

God says:

- Will you go where I send you?
- When my call comes, will you answer?
- Will you leave your comfort and set out to the unknown?
- Will you walk fearlessly into the deep with me?
- Will you go?

Shoot, those are some hard questions. I don't care who you are; these are not easy requests. They come with a cost. When we think about the cost Christ paid for us, one would think "Yes, Lord" would flow from our lips like honey. But it doesn't, and the hesitation is real for all of us.

I think this "go" idea is ironically hard for the West, especially the American culture. Here in America, we go because we can. We have earned it, right? We go when we want, where we want, how we want, with whom we want, and we go our own way. I will add, a very comfortable way too. We have come very accustomed to calling the shots. We are comfortable when we can boldly proclaim our way. It gives us a sense of security when we can control our way. Oh, we of little faith.

We have cultivated a comfy culture for ourselves. Our level of comfort is like none other in the world today. Good, bad, or otherwise, it proves to be a harder go with God when he commands our obedience. We have created this hard go. Hard words to hear.

How do we get accustomed to going with God wherever he calls us go?

I am not sure—in our human, fleshy self—this will never be easy, nor is it supposed to be. We have decided that hard is bad, and easy is good. We live in this mindset, and it trips us up every time. We have decided that to obey is bad. We have made it negative. When we have fully surrendered to live for Christ, obedience isn't bad or negative; it becomes a desire. When we obey Christ, we get to experience Christ in a very intimate way. It is what we long for, and it requires obedience. The adventure awaits our obedience.

Faith is the foundational answer to our living a life in Christ.

* Hard means healthy growth. This requires faith.
* Hard means be on guard, examine oneself, and prepare to be stretched again.
* Faith means adventure awaits with a trusting smile.
* Faith means trusting in something bigger and better than our ideas or our way(s).
* Faith means knowing where he calls me to go, he is there.

- Faith means experiencing peace that passes our understanding in the hard.
- Faith means taking a step into the deep knowing God has our best waiting.
- Faith means questions are not necessary because the answer is on its way.
- Faith is believing the command to go is just exactly where we are supposed to go.
- Faith is what makes the great adventure great.
- Faith means we no longer struggle to show God's love. We discover it's within us. We desire to claim and proclaim the message of Jesus. We have it, we live it, and we give it.

When we can position ourselves in a posture of faith, we will long to go with God wherever he takes us. We will anticipate his call. We will be ready.

His command will be our desire to go on assignment with the gospel for and with our great God.

Lord, let this be so. We pray in Jesus's name.

Let's engage the great adventure, even if it means we go frightened, for he will be there to carry our burden along his way to greatness!

Let's go!

Day 16

Take That Step

Have you ever lost your groove and felt stuck in a funk?

I'm trying to get my groove back again. This means no more sitting on my blessed assurance! So Mia—my four-legged buddy—and I headed out for a walk. *Hate* is a big word that should not be used often, but walking for me, it's close. I really do not like walking, especially if its goal is for health. Walking for well-being can be awesome with the right company, but nope, I just don't like it much. The trees and grass are not enough of a distraction for me, so hubby hooked me up with this Bluetooth gig. I think this is the thing to ease my dislike of walking.

I was listening to a preacher, a good one!

She said something so simple that really grabbed hold of me.

She was referring to Simon and his fishing trip. Do you like to fish? I do if I can catch a fish in the first five minutes in order to keep my attention. I am over it if the fish aren't biting. If it's hot, it's time to dive in and swim. That ruins fishing for everyone with and around me. I don't fish much and shouldn't.

Simon was disappointed too. No fish! I imagine his patience was gone. Add this to his disappointment, and you have a bad combination. I have been there, so I know the ugly that comes with that cocktail.

Simon's career was to fish. He had to know all the tricks to fill that net. He wanted to be done, but Jesus said to Simon after he finished teaching to people on the shore, "Put your net into the deep water."

Simon says, "Jesus, we have fished all night. I am done for the day." But Simon obeyed (key word), and Jesus showed him what only he could do. There was a transformation that happened to Simon that Jesus had planned, and Simon had no idea.

Simon was like, "Dudes, get over here and help me. The boat is sinking because the motherload of fish has been given to us. They were in shock!"

I am thinking they thought Jesus might be the fish whisperer back in the day.

Imagine this happening. You can't make that stuff up. It's true that seeing is believing, and this was the real deal for Simon that day. You don't unsee this.

They came back to shore in a state of many emotions. Simon's life passed before his eyes, and he fell to the ground and repented because his soul was stirred to a place of surrender. This is a key point to the account of Simons fishing trip that day.

Jesus said, "Because I placed these fish in your reach, to believe, you will now become fishers of men."

These guys gave it all up for Jesus and followed him.

From disappointment to divine intervention is what I call this.

- What have you done all day, or for days, that has turned to a disappointment?
- What about that thing you have been working on for weeks, and the result of your hard work falls very short?
- What about that thing you have devoted years to and you haven't seen results? We have all been there. Disappointment and not because of lack of effort. What do we often do in these exhausting seasons?
- Pray for God to make it work.
- Give up and call it "not meant to be."
- Stay focused on it, and try coming at it from an angle.

You can add to this list.

Simon was working hard at his craft.

No doubt Jesus saw Simon's disappointment and hard work without results.

I believe Simon was done for the day. "I'm going home. See ya!" But the Lord was just getting started.

This biblical account is for us just as it was for Simon.

Our disappointment is not usually because of a lack of effort for that thing. We are often really committed to our cause. What becomes the roadblock from achieving results? Simon's story lays this out. Disappointment is the roadblock.

When we become disappointed, a number of things happen.

- Maybe we become so consumed by the disappointment that we don't hear the Lord say, "Get in the boat. Come into the deep with me." Profound.
- We get so taken down by the disappointment that we can't hear a thing. We soon spin our wheels and are stuck. When we get unstuck, we go our own way.
- Maybe we decide to not go into the deep water because we are already drowning and it doesn't make sense, so we refuse to trust the unchartered outcome.
- Or we wait for God to place the missing link in our hand while he holds the other. Our arm gets tired from holding our hand out, and the wait produces doubt. This is a really hard place to be. "Come on, God. I have been faithful, and I need your help."

Okay, this is it! This is what grabbed me.

This is where we too often go wrong in our self-induced disappointments. As a believer, we know that God always has us on the move for his plan and his purpose. So that stuck place should alert every believer that God is about to offer an assignment of sorts.

God will place something in our hands for a rescue or for the answer, to remind us of his promise, or to help us in the wait. He does things like this. If you have experienced it, it brings peace and a sense of relief. God knows when we need to see his hand in our hard.

But God often places our refuge, rescue, or result at our reach. This blows me away. *God places our help in our reach for us to take that step of faith by trusting.*

Simon got in the boat. He took that step. He went to the deep (disappointed), but he knew he needed to go. Obedience.

That abundance of the big catch was his reach. It was there for him, but he had to go and receive and retrieve it. That changed the direction of his life going forward.

That took every bit of his disappointment away.

And what's more important is, what did Simon do after he experienced this abundance?

He followed Jesus to do the work of the Lord, sharing and showing his love to a hurting world, period.

What a great account for us to not only learn by but grow by. I love this and need to be reminded of this. Maybe you do too.

This is what I learned on my dreaded walk today. I'm glad I went.

- Will we checkmark our disappointments right away as a red flag, or see them as part of our assignment or our next best thing God has at our reach?
- Will we be listening for the Lord's invitation to get into the boat?
- Will we go into the deep with Jesus?
- Will we recognize what is at our reach outside our plan and our way?
- Will we see the abundance outside our plan?
- Will we see the abundance God has for us, and drop our agenda and follow him to be fishers of men?

Fishing, anyone?

Day 17

His Voice

Have you ever heard someone say, "The voice of the Lord has been so clear lately!"?

Have you stepped back and felt that pit in your stomach because you wonder if you have ever heard the voice of God, or maybe you don't think you ever have? I think all are very real thoughts among followers of Christ. Our personal journey with Jesus is just that: very personal. It's a relationship that runs deep and is very intimate. God created us for intimate conversation with him.

It's the King of kings who sets up this relationship through his son, Jesus Christ. It's not easily explained. It has to be experienced to be understood. The good news is that it is for everyone who seeks and surrenders.

Each new morning, and in each new season of life, the Father offers a holy invitation to advance us to the next level with him. He invites us to meet with him, to speak to him where his spirit speaks afresh. His voice leads us to places we've never been and to places we need to be.

We have to learn, through holy training and obedience, to believe in the unbelievable.

We have to make peace with obedience.

The world has cheated us by telling us obedience is bondage, but in Christ's economy, it's truly freedom. Obedience isn't a no; it's

God's best yes for us. It swims in an ocean of grace and leads us into freedom, wholeness, and health.

Do we always like obedience? No, double no. Almost never. But when we can surrender to it, we realize it's for *God's* best. This *duty* gives way to *desire*. Obedience becomes something we long to engage with because it means we are experiencing God in a very real way.

Obedience begs a plan. We need an intentional plan of surrender of self and our distractions to be able to hear the voice of God.

It's holy training. This takes practice and positioning ourselves in a constant posture of surrender. In plain English, we have to get our self-made stuff out of the way.

Where will we hear the voice of God most? For sure in the Word of God. We have to stop frantically searching for God's will and start frantically searching for God himself. We will find him in his living Word. If we commit to this practice of being in God's Word, he will use the power of the Holy Spirit to reveal himself there.

It's not this mystical, magical sprinkling that overcomes us. Some churches over emotionalize the work of the Holy Spirit. This has given God a bad name and has disrespected his all-surpassing power.

God never sent his Spirit to confuse. This is not of God.

- We hear the voice of God through the Holy Spirit in us.
- We need to be into the Word of God if we want to hear God's voice. His Word will be brought to mind as the Holy Spirit speaks to us. This is transforming power.

How will we know it's the voice of God?

When we hear the voice of God, it will *always* align with the Word of God.

Don't miss this. If you are never hearing God's voice, get into his Word.

God's voice will never contradict the Bible. If the voice you're hearing is encouraging you to take Scripture out of context to make it fit your situation, that voice isn't of God.

Hearing the voice of God requires obedience to studying the Word of God so we can bring his Word to mind to discern his voice. This can't be said enough.

What voice are we listening to?

There are three voices we will hear:

1. Our own voice speaking over God.
2. The enemy's voice speaking thoughts into our mind. The enemy can't read our minds but is a master of putting thoughts into our minds.
3. God's voice by and through the power of the Holy Spirit.

Discerning which is important. This goes back to the Word of God. Does the voice I am hearing line up to God's Word?

God's voice never contradicts his Word. This reminds us of just how important God's Word is to us. This begs the question for all of us: Are we in God's Word? Or is this saved for Sunday morning only?

Do we have a relationship with the Holy Spirit in us?

When the words jump off the pages of the Bible, that is the working of the Holy Spirit in and to us. That is a great time to stop and listen up because class has begun, and the teacher is speaking. Let's be good students.

This is hearing the voice of God through his Word. Why? Because God's Word is alive! The Holy Spirit opens the door for us to engage and meet with the Lord in this supernatural way.

When we decide to follow Jesus, we become a child of God, born again and anew to living by the power of the Holy Spirit in us. I think we too often miss this part of our salvation.

We might say the salvation prayer and call it being a Christian. We might have a powerful transformation like I did and then say, "Now what?"

The supernatural part (Holy Spirit) is the part two of our salvation that we too often overlook.

Too many times, we:

- Are never taught about this critical reality

- Are confused by the supernatural in us
- Are afraid of him

But when we embrace and become one with the Holy Spirit within us, we then have fully understood our salvation. Until we do, we will too often walk in wonder by a set of rules or walk in a state of unfinished business with God.

The Holy Spirit isn't a foggy haze or something to be feared.

It's what the Lord Jesus left behind for us to walk out this life with. He is our helper and teacher.

When we read the Word of God, it is the Holy Spirit that allows us to comprehend it. We feel the power in the words. We need to cultivate a relationship with the Holy Spirit within us to be able to discern the voice of God.

This supernatural life is surreal but very real. We were created to walk through life in and by this power.

Believe and be saved.

Obey the masters teaching.

Practice holy training.

Discern the voice of God.

> *My sheep hear My voice, and I know them, and they follow Me.* (John 10:27)

> *But the Helper, the Holy Spirit, whom the Father will send in My name, He will teach you all things, and bring to your remembrance all things that I said to you.* (John 14:26)

Day 18

What If...

Did you know, on average, people change jobs every three years? People are really on the move these days. It feels a bit crazy to me. It seems like a lot of work too. We live in an area where people stick tight and cling to their roots. I know people who have never left the state. It would be unthinkable for them to leave their homestead. It's where their life started, and it will end there. Imagine a life built like this. A legacy and built-in traditions. It's safe, comfortable, and secure.

When I was in high school, for me, California was the place to be. I was sure I would end up there. It was my dream. I have lived my life of sixty-plus years, ten minutes from my hometown which is very far from California. I love my cozy little home, and I have made a life there. God has, however, filled my restless ways. He has called me out to many unfamiliar and risky places near and far. It has been an abundant life filled with one adventure after another with him leading the way.

Read this with me:

Now the LORD had said to Abram: "Get out of your country, from your family and from your father's house, to a land that I will show you.

"I will make you a great nation; I will bless you, and make your name great; And you shall be a blessing.

"I will bless those who bless you, and I will curse him who curses you; and in you all the families of the earth shall be blessed."

So Abram departed as the Lord had spoken to him, and Lot went with him. And Abram was seventy-five years old when he departed from Haran. (Genesis 12:1–4)

So Abram departed as the Lord had spoken to him, and Lot went with him. And Abram was seventy-five years old when he departed from Haran. Then Abram took Sarai his wife and Lot his brother's son, and all their possessions that they had gathered, and the people whom they had acquired in Haran, and they departed to go to the land of Canaan. So they came to the land of Canaan. Abram passed through the land to the place of Shechem, as far as the terebinth tree of Moreh. And the Canaanites were then in the land. (Genesis 12:4–6)

This beginning part of Genesis chapter 12 is a bit daunting and bids us to read on—except I got stuck and stunned, so I stopped right there.

The Lord said, *"Leave. Leave it all, your country and your people."* This is a serious gut-wrenching test of faith.

We need to stop here and ask ourselves the obvious question: How would we react, and how would we respond?

God has called me out to go but has never said leave it all. How about you?

Going out and leaving it all are very different. I have been called out to some crazy places with God because I said yes to his to call to go here or there. But that's not leaving. My cozy, comfortable life was always waiting for my return. God said to Abram, "Leave it all behind." It would take a supernatural tug to move that message into action for me. The Bible has been written for you and me. God could call us out to leave too. Are we ready for this?

The story doesn't end there, nor does the shock value for us. The very next part of that verse, the Lord God says, "...*to a land I will show you.*" Read that again. Abram has no clue where he is going! Those two words, "Yes, Lord," are stuck in my throat.

In verse 4, it says, "*So Abram departed as the Lord had instructed him.*"

He goes; he does it! He wanders off into a severe famine and waits it out. He obeyed. Abram was a leader, a husband, and a father going about his life. He was human, so we know this wasn't easy; but he understood that obedience doesn't always come with options.

Is this scripture screaming at you as it has me: "Oh you of little faith"? I want to be like Abram.

- This is the evidence of knowing God and obeying him.
- This is sold-out trusting when things are unclear and make no sense at all.
- This is waiting in the hard, real hard.
- This is saying "Yes, Lord" without pause.
- This is faith-filled obedience.
- God's call was clear, but the destination was not. That's faith—the kind that pleases God.

Abram found that you don't always need to know where you are going if you know who you are following.

This is a big challenge the Lord just wants to hear. "Yes, Lord, I will." This requires blind obedience. If we can get past ourselves, can we just imagine the great adventure with God?

What if…

- God says quit your job and move your family to Africa?
- God says, "Take this couple off the street and have them stay with you until they can get their life back in order"?

- God says to you about the guy you have been dating for five years, "Leave"?
- God says, "I'm going to allow discomfort that will bring you to your knees"?

Are the resounding words to these possibilities "Yes, Lord"?
What if we were like Abram?
What if…

Day 19

Conquering Fear

Fear is a real word in this very fear-filled world.

Have you ever been filled with fear? Not this simmering fear we face today in a world that is falling apart but real paralyzing fear? I had a reoccurring dream for years! I mean like five years. It would come out of nowhere and paralyze me.

The dream was about a grizzly bear pulling my daughter out of her tent and dragging her into the woods. She was screaming and looking at me. Yeah, paralyzing! I can hardly type it out. I would wake up for years, crying, heart racing, sweating, and distraught. It took me hours to recover. So that is the fear I have known. Do you have or have had a crippling fear, or just one that is simmering?

The dream stopped, but not on its own. I had to conquer this irrational fear. How do you stop a monster like this that taunts and disrupts our life? *With the truth.* When I woke up after each night-mare, I began speaking truth in its face. Instead of lying there reliving it or walking it out for hours, I slapped it straight up in the face with the truth. My daughter was alive and well, and the devil is a liar! He doesn't get to rob or steal my joy in the morning because the truth is, joy does come in the morning. The Bible says so, and our great God does not lie.

Weeping may endure for a night, but joy comes in the morning. (Psalm 30:5b)

We have the authority to send the father of lies to the curb every time. We will beat fear by speaking truth that comes from God's Word. Fear will destroy our joy. That is truth too. It hinders our potential with and for God. It's a distraction, and it affects every part of our lives. Our relationships, our family, our daily lives, and most importantly, our relationship with God. The enemy uses fear, and he is very good at it! We see it all around us today. If we unpack our circumstances today, the foundation is too often fear-based.

Fear masquerades itself as something else. The enemy is good at his game. Are we paying attention?

Have we become timid?

Are we feeling more insecure?

How about a lack of confidence?

Do we procrastinate?

We fear the unknown and so easily fall into the enemy's hand. The Lord has not encouraged any of these weaknesses nor placed them in our minds.

But fear not, for we have the authority to fight with the truth.

> *Therefore, submit to God. Resist the devil and he will flee from you.* (James 4:7)

> *Behold, I give you the authority to trample on serpents and scorpions, and over all the power of the enemy, and nothing shall by any means hurt you.* (Luke 10:19)

> *For though we walk in the flesh, we do not war according to the flesh. For the weapons of our warfare are not carnal but mighty in God for pulling down strongholds, casting down arguments and every high thing that exalts itself against the knowledge of God, bringing every thought into captivity to the obedience of Christ.* (2 Corinthians 10:3–5)

Whenever I am afraid, I will trust in You. (Psalm 56:3)

For God has not given us a spirit of fear, but of power and of love and of a sound mind. (2 Timothy 1:7)

I sought the LORD, and He heard me, and delivered me from all my fears. (Psalm 34:4)

Day 20

A Notable Difference

Now when they saw the boldness of Peter and John, and perceived that they were uneducated and untrained men, and then they marveled. And they realized that they had been with Jesus. (Acts 4:13)

These disciples that Jesus chose were a little bit crazy and were very ordinary. When Jesus enlisted them, they were a mess, just like we are. They were vain, fearful, doubting, and never sure of themselves. James and John sought to outmaneuver their fellow disciples in order to gain the places of great honor next to Jesus (Mark 10:37).

Over and over again, the disciples' actions showed that they didn't know who Jesus was (John 6:7–9). Even after three years with Jesus, Peter was still not getting it (Matthew 26:69–75). Anyone who knew these twelve ordinary men would realize they were not the kind of men you would expect to be change agents of the world. Yet something happened to them when they were with Jesus. They were transformed. The Holy Spirit was responsible for this. These disciples became very wise and had a boldness for speaking out about the love of Jesus.

We are not different than those crazy disciples. We are very ordinary, just like they were. Have you spent time with Jesus? Has your heart and mind been transformed like the disciples? Without Christ, we are nothing. With Christ, we are still ordinary people with transformed hearts to do great things for Christ—people will see a notable difference in us.

I come from a small town where everyone knew your name and your game! I was a wild child, full of the wrong kind of adventure. When Christ captured my heart and filled me with the Holy Spirit, there was a notable change. After my transformation, I would run into people I knew from my wild child days, and they were amazed and they marveled. There was a notable difference in me. Some were bold enough to say, "You are a church girl now?" That makes me giggle a little with a grateful heart.

This world tells us ordinary isn't enough, and we can believe it if we don't keep our eyes fixed on the master designer of our redeemed hearts. Sometimes we doubt the transformation within us because it's doesn't show up with lightning bolts and smoke. Because we don't feel it, we get stuck as if we are in sinking sand, losing our confidence and dismissing the power we have within.

Instead of sinking down, pulling back, or pushing forward on our own power, we need to stop and realize that when Jesus took hold of our hearts, he transformed us, giving us a new boldness and wisdom that comes from the Holy Spirit within. We need to walk in a relationship with this master teacher and counselor within. He will guide us and immerse us in his power in order to launch us into a hurting world.

Our job is to go outside of our self and get into the world, into the lives of others, and live for Christ in us. When we do this, everyone around us will see and experience his noticeable difference in our very ordinary lives.

Let our light shine before all so they can see the glorious works in us by and through the powerful Holy Spirit within us.

You are the light of the world. A city that is set on a hill cannot be hidden. Nor do they light a lamp and put it under a basket, but on a lampstand, and it gives light to all who are in the house. Let your light so shine before men, that they may see your good works and glorify your Father in heaven. (Matthew 5:14–16)

Day 21

Hold the line

Read Daniel chapters 1 to 7.

This is a bit of a read but well worth it. Take some time today to check it out.

I grabbed some nuggets from reading this account that had me thinking today. Come with me as I share some insight and encouragement for us today. Staying with Daniel chapters 1 to 7 is like reading an action-packed novel. Because the Bible is inherent, the stories can cause an uncomfortable pause. Chapter 2 gets right down to it: idols and the fiery furnace. The questions surrounding this story for us are:

When all is on the line, who will we worship?

When the moment of choice is looking us in the face, who will we obey?

As a follower of Christ, it's easy for us to jump to the church answers. But I don't believe it's always that simple. These three faithful amigos in this biblical account of the fiery furnace are three we need to pay close attention to today and in the days to come.

The King Nebuchadnezzar was thankful for Daniel's interpretation of his dream, but it didn't change him or his heart. He sounded very positive about Daniel's God, but it was very superficial. How can we know this? Because he didn't waste time creating a ninety-foot golden image. An idol for worship. He didn't put out a city-wide invite to meet at city square for fun fellowship. This is what he said:

"You are commanded, all peoples, nations and languages, that when you hear the sound of the horn, pipe, lyre, trigon, harp, bagpipe, and every kind of music, you are to fall down and worship the golden image the king Nebuchadnezzar has set up."

To make sure that everyone follows his command informs them that "whoever does not fall down and worship shall immediately be cast into a burning fiery furnace." Feels a bit like things are pretty much on the line. In layman's terms, I have put up this amazing image, and I want submission and worship from everyone or else you will die.

And everyone says, "Okay, we will bow." For the follower of Christ, this feels a bit daunting.

But not the three amigos! Remember, they refused to eat what the master commanded and figured a way out. Food or fire, big difference. The stakes have raised.

When the moment of choice is looking at us in the face, what will we do?

What did Daniel and his friends say?

> *Shadrach, Meshach, and Abednego answered and said to the king, "O Nebuchadnezzar, we have no need to answer you in this matter. If that is the case, our God whom we serve is able to deliver us from the burning fiery furnace, and He will deliver us from your hand, O King. But if not, let it be known to you, O King, that we do not serve your gods, nor will we worship the gold image which you have set up. (Daniel 3:16–18)*

For them, this was the beginning and the end for them. They were not going to do it. Why?

Here it is. Because they *believed* in the one true God, and God told them not to do it.

> *You shall not make for yourself a carved image—any likeness of anything that is in heaven*

above, or that is in the earth beneath, or that is in the water under the earth; you shall not bow down to them nor serve them. For I, the LORD your God, am a jealous God, visiting the iniquity of the fathers upon the children to the third and fourth genera-tions of those who hate Me. (Exodus 20:4–5)

They obeyed because they believed, therefore the desire to obey was part of their DNA.

But how did they feel? Can we even imagine? No, we can't, but we can read this account on our knees and ask for this kind of obedi-ence. Obedience most often doesn't feel good, but its reward is worth the discomfort that comes with it.

This king built an idol for himself and forced it onto others. Idolatry is confidence in something other than God to deliver what we need.

We have long lists of idols begging for our worship in this Western world we love and live in.

There are idols we bow down to not because we are made to but because we want to, and those are even harder to acknowledge.

The three amigos said, "No, we will not! Regardless the cost, we will not cave to the narrative or the culture or the agenda. How about us today?

These disciples understood that obedience was attached to their rock-solid stand to say no.

Faith is still obedience despite the consequences.

We are called to obey even

- when it won't work out well for us (that is hard and part of the suffering we can expect according to God's Word)
- when it seems better not to (the world does not compre-hend this)
- when we base our decision-making on what looks more sen-sible or beneficial or understandable. Then when it comes to it, we're going to worship our culture's idols instead of obeying God (looks are deceiving).

The Christian life is sometimes going to look like resisting the attractiveness of an idol; refusing to meet the expectations of everyone else; and accepting the consequences of mockery, authorization, unemployment. And even worse, we are not called to be pragmatic but faithful to say, "God has said this, and so I will do it," like these three amigos.

What will see us hold the line is a simple, straightforward, and unerring obedience to the Word of God even if it means the fiery furnace.

Are we ready?

Day 22

Jesus, take the wheel

Do you get excited when you find out you will be the one to stand on the stage and present? Some people really do get excited. I would say the majority of us get that sick feeling when we find out we will be the person to speak to the masses.

In Athens, the Spirit of God empowered Paul to present the truth of God to an unbelieving audience of Greek philosophers. Standing on Mars Hill, which was viewed as the seat of worldly wisdom, he brilliantly proclaimed God's Word.

However, after his proclamation, he became emotionally shaken. He had prayed that the hearts of those who heard his words would be changed, but his message had received only a lukewarm reception. By the time he sailed for Corinth, he was struggling with discouragement, and God knew it. Therefore, he spoke words of encouragement to his servant:

> *Do not be afraid; keep on speaking, do not be silent. For I am with you, and no one is going to attack and harm you, because I have many people in this city.* (Acts 18:9–10)

In other words, "Paul, you are not alone. I am aware of your circumstances. I am with you, and others who know me are with you too."

Have you ever been there? You have something to say, to share, to proclaim, or to give—and it falls flat! It's a bomb! It's embarrassing! It's a shattering blow!

It might be a conversation with a close friend that you have to have. You've prepared well, but your heart and head disconnect when you begin to speak.

How about when you are in an awkward place standing with a stranger, and you know you need to say something to kill the silence? And you talk about the weather! Obvious bomb.

Or you have to speak in front of a group, you've prepared, and feel 80 percent sure you will kill it in a good way. As you scan your audience, they are not having it, and you have just started.

That was me. I still get sick as I recall the disaster. I needed to share a very important message with some really important, awesome people. I prepared for months. It was a simple message with a powerful message. I don't like speaking in front of people, so I was nervous; but I knew I was supposed to follow through. God said so.

Here is the beginning to the end to my disaster. I didn't feel confident but intimidated. I kept going over and over my notes. As the days drew closer, I got more and more sick. I began thinking, *Maybe I am not supposed to do this.* But God said so. Never a good idea to question God.

So what do you do? I prayed for confidence and a calm. Sometimes God chooses to teach in his answered prayers.

It did not go well. Five minutes into a three-day commitment was a total bomb. Three days of disaster. I didn't give in or give up, but I blew it for sure. A very humbling not-so-fun ordained ordeal.

I fumbled and I was a sweaty mess. I thought I might lose my cookies. Have you been here?

I remember locking eyes with my hubby, my safe place. Poor guy was freaking out for me.

My confidence was beyond crushed! I tried really hard to build myself up and gather my thoughts to remember the important message to be shared. I realized the message was still good. It was me; it was my confidence.

I learned a really big lesson in that disaster. This is it: *I didn't bring Christ.* I didn't ask him to lead the way, to speak through me. I planned, prepared, and panicked on my own; and I fell flat on my face.

I learned that when I am given an assignment, I am not expected to go at it alone. God is there to walk me through the planning and the presentation. At that moment, I realized that nothing changed, but everything changed. I still have the assignment and the hard work to prepare and practice, but I wasn't alone and was not working it out alone.

I still really do not like speaking in front of people, and it took me awhile to give it another go; but I go differently now. I remind myself:

Do not be afraid, keep on speaking, do not be silent, but bring Christ with me.

> *And I am sure of this, that he who began a good work in you will bring it to completion at the day of Jesus Christ.* (Philippians 1:6)

It still takes courage, and I still go frightened; but I try always to look up, give a thumbs-up, and thank Jesus for taking control! I give it all up to God before I speak a word. I ask him to speak through me.

We are always learning, aren't we? I want to be a good student because I have the best teacher!

> *However, when He, the Spirit of truth, has come, He will guide you into all truth; for He will not speak on His own authority, but whatever He hears He will speak; and He will tell you things to come.* (John 16:13)

> *Have I not commanded you? Be strong and of good courage; do not be afraid, nor be dismayed, for the LORD your God is with you wherever you go."* (Joshua 1:9)

And the L<small>ORD</small>, He is the One who goes before you. He will be with you; He will not leave you nor forsake you; do not fear nor be dismayed. (Deuteronomy 31:8)

Day 23

Ticktock

Eighty-six thousand four hundred seconds that we never get back. That is how many seconds each one of us get each day to use up. How have you used your seconds today? Once gone, they are gone, not to recover or relive again. Time waits for no one. When we stop long enough to look at time, it is sobering. It makes one think: What do I need, could, or should be doing?

When we are young, we are very busy managing time. As we get older, time becomes a tender word, as we realize how little we have. I am in that older category today and have realized that I am on the other side of the mountain. I've entered the downhill side. I can let that depress me, or I can see it as the most amazing downhill ride I will ever get to ride.

Some years ago, my husband and I did the superman zip line ride in Costa Rica. It was daunting. The ride up the mountain to the start point was sickeningly scary. Sitting in an old rickety open-sided jeep that sounded like it needed a tune up was unnerving. As for someone who is afraid of heights, this was a sweaty risk. The knot in my stomach tightens as I type this.

People say, "If it was so scary, why did you do it?" The answer is simply hard. I didn't want to miss a moment. And…I didn't. I pulled up my big girl pants and literally flew like superwoman through the sky. I will never regret it.

It proved a couple things to me. We fight our fears by asking two questions: What is real? What is true? When these questions are answered, we almost always have the freedom to fly! I am learning to take on moments in time because once they are gone, we can't get them back. This life here on Earth is very short.

As a follower of Christ, when this life here ends, we graduate to paradise—to a perfect forever. This is the gift to all who believe in the birth, life and death, and resurrection of Jesus Christ. Salvation is a sweet gift and ticket to forever.

But that isn't today, so what do we do with these eighty-six thousand seconds each day. The question is: How will we make the most of God's gift of time?

Our eighty-six thousand seconds each day is the dress rehearsal for the forever banquet table we are invited to. The only thing the invitation is missing is: *When?*

Being our best for his glory gives us the very best adventure with each breath we take for the seconds we get to live.

Make today a big blessing!

Day 24

Rejoice by Faith

Have you found yourself in a gloomy place—a place where the pain is too much to take, where the struggle doesn't let up, or where a dark cloud seems to lead you around?

We have all been in these places. We all have a story to go with the struggles we have endured.

If we look into the Book of 1 Peter 1:6–7, God's Word has some encouragement for us in these hard times that none of us will escape on this side of heaven. Read the verse here with me, and then let's break it down to see the hope in our hard times.

> *In this you greatly rejoice, though now for a little while, if need be, you have been grieved by various trials, that the genuineness of your faith, being much more precious than gold that perishes, though it is tested by fire, may be found to praise, honor, and glory at the revelation of Jesus Christ.* (1 Peter 1:6–7)

Verse 6:

> *In this you greatly rejoice, though now for a little while, if need be, you have been grieved by various trials…* (1 Peter 1:6)

It begins with: "*We greatly rejoice in all of this for a little while.*" *Rejoice* means "to praise God."

We are to praise God in and for our struggles and trials? That just doesn't feel right, but if we believe in this God of great mercy, we can rejoice. Why?

When we realize our ability to cope in the present is tied to our understanding of our inheritance in the future, we can rejoice. If we cannot make the link between the now (trials and suffering) and the not yet (eternal glory), grace won't be multiplied on our lives. Does this make sense? When it does, it makes the struggle somehow less.

Anchored. I love this word! I think about a boat that is tipping and being tussled by roaring, turbulent waves during a storm. If the boat is anchored to the bottom of the lake, it will still get ugly and hard to maintain stability, but it's got a firm foundation holding it in place. It's secure.

In our time of trouble, in our storms in this life, we have a firm foundation in Christ who doesn't leave us to fight the storm alone. He is our anchor. The storms will come, but he will never leave.

There is an expiration date on our trials regardless of how big or small as Winston Churchill says: "If you find yourself going through hell, get through it."

For the Christ follower comes the bonus: we never go through our struggle alone because our God promises to never leaves us.

People leave the church and their faith because they find it impossible to believe that a good God would allow us to suffer.

The truth is, it is impossible for the human mind to grasp this kind of love. This is where we must surrender to living by faith. When we decide our thoughts and ways are not God's, then we will be able to rejoice still.

"If you find yourself going through hell, get through it." Fight the right fight, for your future is final as a follower of Christ.

Why does trouble await each of us if God only wants his best for us? Someone has to be responsible.

We will wrestle with this, especially in the storm, so plan on it in advance so your faith will rise up in the right time.

> *The thief does not come except to steal, and to kill, and to destroy. I have come that they may have life, and that they may have it more abundantly.* (John 10:10)

> *Be sober, be vigilant; because your adversary the devil walks about like a roaring lion, seeking whom he may devour.* (1 Peter 5:8)

That's why. Trouble awaits because we have a ready and willing enemy who is relentless.

The enemy will attack; and if we aren't careful, cautious, prayed up, and suited up, the enemy will cause havoc in our lives. Sin is part of this life on Earth, and trouble is sure to show up for each of us. Trouble comes with this life, but we have the remedy and the fix. We have Christ in us, fighting for us with each struggle we face.

This trouble talked about in verse 6 is, "*But for a short time.*" Our expiration date is real too!

For a short time (that expiration date thing), we will suffer. This is true, but help in hard times is our supernatural faith.

The supernatural part is what we must come to terms with. We cannot fight on our own. We must surrender to it because it is living within the follower of Christ. *Surrender* is a big, hard word, but it is the answer to living this life fearlessly out loud.

Walking by and in faith is a supernatural adventure we don't want to miss out on.

Faith sets us on a path that no matter comes our way, there is no going back, and we will go through fire to live in the supernatural with our Savior.

To one who has faith, no explanation is necessary. To one without faith, no explanation is possible.

> *But without faith it is impossible to please Him, for he who comes to God must believe that He is, and that He is a rewarder of those who diligently seek Him.* (Hebrews 11:6)

Day 25

Go and Do What He Did

The expert on the law answered, "The one who showed him mercy." Jesus said to him, "Then go and do what he did." (Luke 10:37)

I've got it!

What do you know about volleyball? Did or do you play volleyball? It's a fun sport. I played many moons ago. Our daughters were very good volleyball players in high school. Shannon was precise in setting the ball to her sister, and Lindsey knew how to slam it down. They were a force to be reckoned with. I so miss watching them. Oh man, it still gets me all fired up! Yup, I was one of those crazy parents in the stand embarrassing their daughters. No regrets! Proud mama here.

But that game requires clasping one's hands and going for the ball. Maybe you have seen this—"I got it" in unison. All players are ready to go after the ball that is sailing over the net. And then (you know what's coming) *thud...* The ball hits the floor with a team standing there postured and ready, but nobody steps into action—not a stellar moment in volleyball. If you know or played the game, you can feel the defeat right there.

My devotion today is titled "The Ball is in Your Court."

"Who will go?" the Lord said to Isaiah.

The assignment is right before us. Are we postured in position to go?

"Yes, Lord, send me."

How many times has ball hit the floor with a thud leaving feeling defeated and convicted?

How many times have we accepted the assignment and walked off the court with joy and victory?

We are sent onto God's court every single day to accompany and accomplish great things with the Lord. There is also a team of those who do not want us to win! They will throw darts at us that will enter our space with great power to distract and cause us to retract if we aren't equipped and confident against all odds.

We will always have a choice. Will we step up, move forward, and nail it, or will hesitate and stand back? Why do we hesitate?

She is far more qualified to take this on.

He is far more prepared.

She has been trained longer than I have.

It's not in my lane. Her personality is a better fit.

Wait, but God gave me the assignment. Who am I to decide I am not good enough?

When we do this, we are in a way telling God he doesn't know what he is doing or that he is making a mistake. Are you feeling the poke of conviction like I am?

God knows exactly what he is doing and won't always give us the details. Why? Because he is patient and will wait for us to lose ourselves and gain great things by obeying his call to his assignment for us. He is waiting for us to say "I got it" and to go.

The Lord knows our soft spot and softens our heart toward the assignment. It's an opportunity to engage. It's our invitation to respond and join him where he is already at work. The Lord is never sending us out on our own. He is already at the net waiting for us to boldly come and nail it!

Isaiah himself felt uniquely unqualified for such a spiritual assignment, yet here I am.

I've got it!

What is our assignment today or tomorrow? It's there; the ball is in our court.

Let's clasp our hands, set our feet firmly, and go for it! Let's go!

> Each of you should use whatever gift you have received to serve others, as faithful stewards of God's grace in its various forms. (1 Peter 4:10)

> Then I heard the voice of the Lord saying, "Whom shall I send? And who will go for us? And I said, "Here am I, send me." (Isaiah 6:8)

Day 26

Change

You are holding a blank sheet of paper in your hands. No big deal, just a blank sheet of paper. You are told to write the word *change* on it. This could now become a big deal. Change can be a very scary word, or one that raises our eyebrow to anticipation. It depends on who we are and what that change writes on our hearts.

One thing is for sure: change comes with many unknowns. I don't think the change is an issue; it's the unknown because our need to control is taken from us. In a time of change, the unknown becomes known step-by-step.

Do you like the element of surprise? Like when you walk into a room and everyone is there to celebrate you. Or you are heading to an unknown destination. Maybe you are blindfolded and someone is leading you somewhere. How does this make you feel?

We are all different. I tend to see unknown destinations as an adventure. Being surprised as I enter a roomful of people to celebrate me isn't an adventure, as I do not like attention on me. Is there such a thing as an excited dread? I love the people and celebration idea, but the surprise on me, not so much. How about you?

This blank sheet of paper of change written on it can be followed by "What if?" Anything could happen.

We all know that living in this world means changes we are called upon to deal with.

Many of the changes we have experienced have been hard and unexpected. A family member passes away suddenly. This brings a big change to deal with. Your job changes and takes you to a new one across the world. This brings a new life to deal with. We have all faced the reality of change in our lives. As we look at the world today, change is happening every day, and we have choices to make as we navigate each new day.

When we face change, choices are required. This can be really intimidating because sometimes our choices lead us to unknown and unchartered places.

We don't have to panic because we don't have to face change alone. We have the master designer of all things to help us wade through every change we must deal with. God is the way maker, and his Word was written by design to give the answers, encouragement, and direction we need to fill our blank page.

So be strong and courageous! Do not be afraid, and do not panic before them. For the Lord your God will personally go ahead of you. He will neither fail you nor abandon you. (Deuteronomy 31:6)

Those words are a game changer because:

Little children, you are from God and have overcome them, for he who is in you is greater than he who is in the world. (1 John 4:4)

If you believe this, it's because:

All Scripture is breathed out by God and profitable for teaching, for reproof, for correction, and for training in righteousness. (2 Timothy 3:16)

When the Spirit of truth comes, he will guide you into all the truth, for he will not speak on his own authority, but whatever he hears he will speak, and he will declare to you the things that are to come. (John 16:13)

For those who live by these words, know that no matter what comes or goes, God is still there and is ever present. When change is pressing upon us, we can have peace over panic, patience over procrastination, calm over chaos, joy over the jitters, and love in the midst of change.

Why? Because:

> *And the LORD, He is the One who goes before you. He will be with you, He will not leave you nor forsake you; do not fear nor be dismayed.* (Deuteronomy 31:8)

We need the Lord in our corner, for trouble is sure to come.

> *But may the God of all grace, who called us to His eternal glory by Christ Jesus, after you have suffered a while, perfect, establish, strengthen, and settle you. To Him be the glory and the dominion forever and ever. Amen.* (1 Peter 5:10–11)

The follower of Christ keeps their eyes fixed forward, for the best is yet to come.

> *For here we have no continuing city, but we seek the one to come.* (Hebrews 13:14)

> *And if I go and prepare a place for you, I will come again and receive you to Myself, that where I am, there you may be also.* (John 14:3)

So then in this ever-changing world and in our ever-changing choices and decisions before us, we know we are being held close by a God who never changes.

While we wait on his glorious return:

> *Watch, stand fast in the faith, be brave, be strong.* (1 Corinthians 16:13)

Our blank page is about full; would you agree?
This is refreshing! It's renewing and reliable.
Let's choose change with confidence.

Day 27

The World's Gold or God's Glory

By the world's standard, gold is anything we treasure, anything that competes with our affection for Jesus Christ.

Whatever you and I value more than God can be considered our gold. According to the Bible, anything we place above or before God in our lives is an idol.

What's your gold? I would rather not share my gold, but it's good for my soul to do so. I don't covet much. My hubby would agree I'm a pretty cheap date. Give me a big juicy hamburger, and I am a happy lady. I don't need fancy clothes or a fancy house, but my car—that darn car—is my weakness. I like a nice car. I have no idea where this came from. I also admit I continue to fail in this area. My gold is a very shiny, white, well-made, and fast car. Father, forgive me.

If you watch TV, the devil dangles golden carrots with every commercial we watch. We can even invest in gold today to live our guaranteed best life. Secular prosperity at its best! The gimmicks are all around us.

To invest in things that eternally matter, we must turn our back on the gold of this world and chase after a gold that lasts.

The Moses of the Bible is a grand example for us. It was by faith with obedience that Moses turned his back on the gold of a very privileged life in Egypt as the adopted son of Pharaoh. If we live in America today, we fully understand a privileged life.

Moses was a man of decision. Throughout his life, he faced hard decisions that would shape his life. You and I are not different. We all know about those hard and hefty decisions we've had to make.

Just like Moses, we are called to make firm (not wishy-washy) decisions. When we do, we are cutting off all other courses of action.

Have you walked it out a firm, well-thought-out, and discerned decision? I have too. It feels good. It comes with power, and it's bold! It's a yes and amen!

Have we walked hard-and-convicting decisions halfway that didn't feel quite as good? We were weak on fulfilling the entire decision because it was too hard. We all have been there too.

Moses lived to be 120 years old. Moses's life can be divided into three segments of forty years. Each of these forty years were marked by major decisions.

- Moses spent the first forty years in the rich palace of Pharaoh learning that he was something and somebody.
- Moses spent the second forty years in the desert learning that he was a nothing and a nobody.
- Moses spent his final forty years leading the Israelites out of Egypt and through the desert. It was there he learned that God is everything.

Moses's story is worth the read (Exodus, Leviticus, Deuteronomy, and Numbers).

The progression of decisions in Moses's life were not by chance. They shaped him and brought him to the end of himself to realize that God was the gold he needed because it was God's glory.

Moses decided to spend the rest of his life seeking not gold but the glory of God. At times he was fearful and he was reluctant, yet he made a decision each time that cut off all other options. He decided to follow the Lord. What did Moses give up?

He gave up everything that stood in the way of faithful obedience. We want to cower because this is hard stuff. But let's remember that obedience is an honor we get to give our great God. The enemy is very alive and well and willing to take us on a detour to a slippery slope if we allow him to.

In America, this world offers to us everything. Fame, its gated glory, wealth, costly supplements to ultimate health, and comfort with a cause too. We live in a very appealing and tricky culture where that golden carrot is around every corner.

If we take the world's bait, we will enjoy its poison for a time; but its temporary thrill loses its luster. Eventually a car reaches the distance of three hundred thousand miles.

After that first forty years of Moses life, he was living the best life with the rich Pharaoh. He had the best of best and lived a lavish life.

The next forty years, he had nothing. The golden carrot was dangling for Moses too. When it got tough, Moses didn't go soft. He remained steadfast.

The first eighty years of Moses's life was holy training for Moses to realize the gold was about living to give God all the glory.

What decision does it require for us to walk out our lives, choosing God's glory over the world's gold?

It requires *authentic* faith. Authentic is the key word here. Authentic faith isn't just words; it's a piercing, firm decision that doesn't and won't always feel good. It's a firm decision that comes with walking through the hard stuff with unshakable obedience to say no to worldly gold and the voices who hold it in their hands.

We can find ourselves in that hard place, declaring, "I don't have a big faith." It's not our way out because God doesn't require our faith to be big. The faith of a mustard seed is enough. But our faith must be *real*.

When we bring our authentic faith to the foot of the cross, no matter the size, God will take us to the gold he has prepared and provided for us in order to bring to him all the glory.

According to God's Word, faith is the willingness to let God rule supreme in every situation. Authentic faith says, "Have thine own way, Lord."

Authentic faith agrees with John the Baptist who said, "He must increase, but I must decrease."

Throughout the Bible, the word *faith* is interchangeable with the word *obedience*. You cannot have one without the other. Faith requires obedience, and obedience requires faith.

As we walk through this life, we will face many decisions.

The choosing will be ours.

God's glory—the world's gold

Day 28

I Promise

A promise is only as good as the one who makes it.

How often have we said, "I promise I will be there!"? It would be on our calendar, and we wait for the day with anticipation. The word *promise* feels stamped without condition. "I will be there. I promise." We have the very best of intentions because our promises mirror our character. How good are we at keeping our word?

And then…it happens. One of the kids get sick, we can't get a sitter, and hubby is working late. I get COVID for the fourth time! An extended family issue comes up, or our job keeps robbing our time. The truth is, our best intentions are often squashed. Our promises are too often broken, and we feel frustrated, sad, and disappointed in ourselves.

We should really stop using that word, *promise*, because everything we do and say come with conditions that can be out of our control. It's unfair for us to guarantee a promise because too often they are broken due to life's unexpected interruptions.

It's only God that brings unconditional promises to our lives. This is a big deal for the believer. When is the last time you sat down and reflected upon God's promises? We too often are completely unaware of the gift of God's promises playing out in our lives.

His promises come with divine power, comfort, and strength; and they always come through. Nothing can interrupt God's promises. God's promises are precious and magnificent, and they are for us. God's promises take our breath away when we experience the gift of them in our lives.

There are too many promises from God to pen here, but one comes to mind that is profound.

> *Be strong and courageous. Do not be afraid or terrified because of them, for the Lord your God goes with you; he will never leave you nor forsake you.* (Deuteronomy 31:6)

This is a foundational verse from Christ to us. Do we really believe this promise? I don't think we do fully. I think distractions pull us away. I think hardship and emotional pain derail us.

Committing to believing the promises from God changes everything for us. His promises bring security, peace, comfort, and confidence into our lives. We will live differently, and boldly walk through life when we claim his promise over our lives.

What if we fully committed to studying the book of God's promises?

- What if we claimed them daily?
- What if we called upon them in our times of need or otherwise?

We would then experience the divine power, strength, peace, comfort, guidance, and love that come with the promises of God.

How about we take a walk through God's Word and reflect upon God's promises for us?

Let's commit to believing in God's promises, claim them over our lives, and call upon our Father when we need him.

Let's be intentional and aware as God pours out his promises into our lives.

God will never break a promise he pours over us. Let us bow down and worship this King.

Day 29

Be Kind

And be kind to one another, tenderhearted,
forgiving one another, even as God in Christ forgave
you. (Ephesians 4:32)

This word from the Bible sounds so beautiful and simple...in a perfect world, right? Being kind and tenderhearted to those we dislike or those who are different from us is uncomfortable and awkward. It's easier to walk on by than stop and check in with that person sitting alone on the park bench. It's easier to snap back not-so-nice words at the person who goes off on us for taking their parking spot.

The verse ends with, "even as God in Christ forgave you." This causes a pause, as it should. I don't know about you, but God is very patient with me when I mess up and when I am not my best. He wants us to show this grace to others because it is given to us.

How do we do this? We don't do this on our own. In our humanness, we fail because we can't love others the way Christ loves us. We must ask for Christ's love to be poured out through us to all those who cross our paths. Be ready because it can be one of the best adventures of our life.

Being kind and compassionate is tricky because if we are going to be, it can't be weak or fake. People see through *an attempt* to be kind. To be genuine is to put God's love into action.

I remember serving dinner at the sober living center, and one of the guys was sitting alone. At this moment, I knew God had an assignment for me, as I felt his nudge. I had some time, so I went and sat down by him. I had no idea how much he just needed someone to sit there. I needed to get up and get something, and he immediately said, "Are you going to come back and sit down?"

Kindness and compassion change people's hearts. I couldn't wait to come back and sit with him. We talked and laughed for about half an hour. We had some pretty serious and deep conversations too. He had things that he needed to process. So that is we did. I had no idea how much he needed someone to just stop. Just stop without an agenda and *be* present with kindness and be compassionate.

He made a comment before I had to leave. He said, "You know, you can tell when someone really cares." His hard heart began to soften that night because of simple kindness and compassion.

I love those assignments from God, and I love my new friend. I thanked the Lord all the way home and prayed for my new friend.

My little children, let us not love in word or
in tongue, but in deed and in truth. (1 John 3:18)

True genuine love is not passive. It actively shows itself. It can't help but pour out onto others.

To be kind and compassionate isn't always comfortable, but it's not an option if we want to receive the blessings that come from taking the risk. It will always be worth the risk.

We must choose to love the way God loves.

A challenge for us today: ask for an assignment.

Be kind. Be compassionate. Look for that person who is alone or the one who needs a helping hand. When you feel that nudge, don't stand back: step forward. Take the risk.

Ask the Lord to help love them the way only he can.

A kind gesture can reach a wound that only
compassion can heal. (Steve Maraboli)

Day 30

The Content Life

Cleansing and contentment go together. I have never given this much thought. Have you? That hot sweaty day when we finally are able to climb in the shower. It feels so good. That is cleansing that leads to contentment.

How about all those weeds choking off our beautiful flowers, cleansing (de-weeding) to contentment? If you are a gardener, you know what this feels like.

How about those baby baths! The best. We gently wash their bodies and fuzzy hair. We dry and lotion them, and then we smell and snuggle them. There is nothing like it: contentment.

Something so simple as that crusted burnt on fry pan. When it shines back at us, contentment.

That mile-high pile of laundry that shows up weekly. When we fold clean clothes and put those last pieces away, contentment.

Cleansing requires doing something, removing something. Typically, this means doing things we aren't very excited to do. It can include hard and many times uncomfortable work.

But the result, that moment of exhale, is so soothing and settled. It's a good place to rest and relax even if just for a moment. That is contentment.

Cleansing and contentment play a consistent and necessary role in the life of the follower of Jesus Christ.

Even the holiest believer is still a sinner. Our full and complete contentment won't be fully experienced until we are in heaven.

Living in holy righteousness is the desire for every believer. Even in our holiness, we get dirty. We all fall short and off the path we have been set upon. Holiness requires cleansing in order to experience the sweet contentment we have in Christ. There is wholeness in holiness when we cleanse ourselves. This is a reach for purity. Holding tight to sin takes us down. It steals our joy, and only God can cleanse so we can rest in contentment. There is nothing like it.

When we come to the feet of Jesus and lay our sin there, we can almost hear the Lord speak to us. "Go now and sin no more." Do we realize what a loving and patient God we serve? If we are seeking contentment, we find ourselves at the feet of our savior more often than we care to admit. Each time, in his loving tender kindness, he takes our sin from us, and it is no more. He sends us back out to be a kingdom worker for his glory. Yes, we will continue to sin, and yes, he will continue to forgive us and send us out. What an amazing God we serve!

Have you experienced a cleansing from Christ? Have you experienced this contentment?

Now godliness with contentment is great gain.
(1 Timothy 6:6)

If we confess our sins, He is faithful and just to forgive us our sins and to cleanse us from all unrighteousness. (1 John 1:9)

Day 31

Stuck

After a number of years, being *stuck* outside of my control and having to make constant adjustments in how I would do life have been challenging, not gonna lie. Have you been there too?

There were times when I could see and feel the *stuck* lifting, which created a different adjustment that ignited excitement. And then, the next *thing* happens, and I was stuck again. It can be very busy being stuck. It's a time of managing the *un*expected, *un*wanted, and *un*asked for, which can send us on the slip and slide to *un*done. Have you been there too? How we manage our messy lives matters.

It can feel like you are either sitting in a mud puddle waiting for the sun to come out because the son is the Savior in our surrender (pun intended). Or it can feel like quicksand sucking the life right out of you. That is the ugly about being stuck.

How do we get through the stuck? I am still in the process and have had a lot of time to think about unexpected messy places we find ourselves in. You might know what I am talking about.

My motto has always been, "This too shall pass," and it does; but recently, it just passes to the next hard thing. A new motto was brought to my attention lately that rings true as well: "If you are going through hell, get through it." And I have recently read, if you are at your wit's end, on your last nerve or dangling at the end of that rigid rope, the Lord is right there. The truth is, he is right there from the start of the stuck and in the midst of it too. He is the glue that catches us when we have exhausted our own resources and have gotten too tired of battling by ourselves.

I have had time in God's classroom, and his peace has carried me through the rough spots, taught me some necessary lessons, and stayed close to the downright ugly.

The holy classroom has a really special place. It's a quiet place in our mind to rest in his peace. This is not the peace of mind we think of. It's a deep soul peace that surpasses our understanding. I believe it's the only way we can walk through these valleys and stay intact.

The Bible is full of God's words that launch us to this quiet place where peace replaces panic and places us in God's presence where we will be content in all circumstances. The valleys were never meant for us to walk alone.

If you are stuck in that hard place, there is hope in the hard. If we can keep Christ in first place leading us through the trials and tribulations that we will face, we will still struggle, we will get weary, and the burden will still be heavy, but the landing is soft if we will choose to rest in the love, peace, joy, and comfort of the Lord.

I have told you these things, so that in me you may have peace. In this world you will have trouble. But take heart! I have overcome the world. (John 16:33)

Fear not, for I am with you; be not dismayed, for I am your God; I will strengthen you, I will help you, I will uphold you with my righteous right-hand. (Isaiah 41:10)

Have I not commanded you? Be strong and courageous. Do not be frightened, and do not be dismayed, for the Lord your God is with you wherever you go. (Joshua 1:9)

Count it all joy, my brothers, when you meet trials of various kinds, for you know that the testing

*of your faith produces steadfastness. And let stead-
fastness have its full effect, that you may be perfect
and complete, lacking in nothing.* (James 1:2–4)

*You keep him in perfect peace whose mind is
stayed on you, because he trusts in you.* (Isaiah 26:3)

*In peace I will both lie down and sleep; for
you alone, O Lord, make me dwell in safety.* (James
1:2–4)

*For there is a moment in his anger;
there is a lifetime in his favor.
Weeping lodges for the evening,
but in the morning comes rejoicing.* (Psalms 30:5)

*May the God of hope fill you with all joy and
peace in believing, so that by the power of the Holy
Spirit you may abound in hope.* (Romans 15:13)

Amen.

Day 32

Hell, No!

Why don't we talk much about hell? Why don't we believe in it? I think the answers are pretty clear.

Belief and fear are responsible for both.

We don't talk about it much in or out of the church because it's horrifically real, and we would rather talk about the love of God instead. What we miss in doing this is that talking about hell speaks loud and clear to God's love for us. Have we ever stopped to look at hell from this view? I believe our lives depend on these discussions.

It's reasonable that if you don't believe in God, you wouldn't speak of hell. That makes sense. But the reality of that, too, is horrific. The broad definition of *hell* is "a place of conscious torment after death." That right there is the scariest thing any human can hear. I don't care who or what we believe, that sentence is scary. Because after death comes eternity. It's a very long time, as in forever long, somewhere.

Do we know that Jesus spent more time warning people about the dangers of hell than He did in comforting them with the hope of heaven? God knows all things and does not want anyone to go to this place that is very real.

We don't and can never claim to have all the answers, but if we believe in God and His Word, then we can better understand the reality of hell.

One fair question is, Did God create hell? If he did, why?

We have to take a walk through the Word to have the Holy Spirit speak the truth that is found there.

Hell is a place of suffering originally prepared by God for the devil and his angels (Matthew 18:9, 25:41).

There are other words associated with hell in the Bible such as Hades (Greek), Sheol (Hebrew), Gehenna, and lake of fire. It is clear that there is an actual place where the spirits of the unsaved go for eternity (Revelation 9:1, 20:15; Matthew 23:33).

Everything that ever was or is or will be is created by God, including hell (Colossians 1:16). John 1:3 says, "All things were made through him, and without him was not anything made that was made." God alone has the power to cast someone into hell (Luke 12:5). Jesus holds the keys to death and Hades (Revelation 1:18).

Jesus said that hell was prepared for Satan and the demons (Matthew 25:41). It is a just punishment for the wicked one.

Hell wasn't created for you and me; it was created for Satan and his tribe.

However, 2 Peter 2:4–9 has a message for all of God's creation.

Hell, or the lake of fire, will also be the destination for those who reject Christ.

We get to choose, and that is a gift for each one of us!

If we go to hell, we have sent ourselves there based on choice. We can't blame a bad God. He wants you and me to live in paradise one day. That has been his plan from the beginning. We want to change the rules when things don't feel right or fit well into our space.

If you think this is just stupid talk, it's your choice, but what if it's true and hell is real? Why would anyone risk this? If hell is real, there is no way back, no second chances. This boggles my mind!

Maybe it makes my head spin because, for a good part of my life, I thought this whole God and the heaven-and-hell thing was stupid. I have lived both lives. There is no shadow of a doubt that God is real, and so are heaven and hell if you have lived on both sides of the track. It becomes very real. Do I understand it all? No, that would be impossible. God's thoughts and ways are not mine. When we can make peace with this, a new life awaits us.

I was a wild child. I did a lot of free thinking and reckless and fun things. I experienced the superb and sketchy things of the world. Today, I live in the supernatural life of surrender.

The bottom line is this: Sin is sexy. It's curious, and chasing after it is fun—really fun—until it's not. Losing our identity and integrity because of our choices is not fun. Giving up self-esteem for a lack of self-control and too many lust-filled nights is not fun for long. The consequences are very real. Looking in the mirror after the dazzle from the mind-numbing drugs dies down is a reality and not a fun one. Addiction is very real, and that battle means facing the giants. This is why people struggle to live with a clear mind. The person in the mirror needs to be reckoned with, and I believe there is only one way. His name is Jesus, and his power comes with the Holy Spirit.

The fact is, it's all fun and games and freedom until we are no longer free but tied up in bondage by our own sinful, scandalous choices.

You might say or be thinking, "I didn't live that life, and my life is good just the way it is. I wouldn't want anything else. I make good choices and do the right things. I work hard and treat people well. I take care of myself and others." That is amazing! You are a hard worker for sure. You have a lot to be proud of because making good choices doesn't always come easy.

This is true in the case of Christ too.

Yes, it's about choices. It will always come down to choices, the good, the bad, and the ugly.

Regardless of how we have chosen to live our lives, we will still die. That is a choice we don't get to make. Death is certain, and fear is a liar.

I know that God is very real and shutter when I think about hell as it was my eternal place before Christ captured my attention and then my heart. I wasn't looking for God at all. He decided to show up and make himself known to me. The choice wasn't hard when I experienced love I had never known. You can't ask me to explain it because it's not of this world. Life with Christ is not of this world. We must live in the world, but we are not of it.

I heard of that being said so often and never quite got it. The words felt twisted somehow.

You don't know what you don't know.

I didn't know what I didn't know, but today, I know, and I'm living proof of the great adventure with God. You might be singing hallelujah with me! You might be caught off guard or confused by it all.

Hell is real, and God loves us so much that he gave up his one and only son to die for us—for all of us—that if we would believe, we could live in eternity. It's a place that we can't outlive—a place that has been prepared for us for those who choose to believe.

It's so worth the risk. It's forever after all is said and done.

Have you ever thought about this God thing, or have you maybe given up on him? Today might be the day to reconsider. You really have little to lose but so much more to gain.

Look at me, a very wild child. Who would have thought? One day, maybe sooner than we think, every knee will bow. We *get* to choose the fork in the road.

Today is a great day to choose Christ.

> *For God so loved the world, that he gave his only begotten Son, that whosoever believeth in him should not perish, but have everlasting life.* (John 3:16)

Day 33

Let's Go!

Have you felt like you were on a gerbil wheel or like a dog chasing its tail? Round and round we go. We get exhausted but make little ground or progress. Or what about that mountain we keep circling? That big one. No, it's huge, and around every curve, we encounter more cliffs and peaks. It makes me weary writing this. If you've been there or are, you feel the weariness that comes with this burden.

Sometimes it's a very long journey from Egypt to the Promised Land in our lives.

But when the fog lifts, we quickly change our mindset and begin to live differently. We have a new lease on life. The dizzy merry-go-ride ends, and we are on our way to something better, something new, and something that we've looked forward to or worked really hard for.

What happens when that eleven-day trip to our promised land turns into forty days? Have you been on this road too? There is good news for all of us. The good news is that no matter how long we've wandered in the wilderness, no matter how long we've been stuck going around the same mountain, God has a better tomorrow and a brighter future planned. All we need is a bit of encouragement to make that final push for that breakthrough to a better place.

Think about Moses who is estimated to have brought two to three million people out of slavery. God's plan was not exactly what he expected. Have you ever been plugging along with *the plan*, feeling it was clear and well laid out, and boom, nothing feels clear at all as everything appears to fall apart? Not a fun place to be. Our faith is tested in big ways during these big delays and detours. True faith tells us that these detours are divine appointments to experience God in powerful ways as we wander in the unknown and unchartered places. What seems to be falling apart may be very well falling right into place. It's very hard to get around this when our self-made world begins to crumble.

When Pharaoh let the people go, God did not lead them on the road through the Philistine country though that was shorter. Did you know this? For God said, "If they face war, they might change their minds and return to Egypt." So God led the people around by the desert road toward the Red Sea (Exodus 13:17–18).

Their delay and detour had a purpose, and so does ours, every time. Let's believe this in the hard middle.

Their delay, long delay, was part of his plan to get them safely to their destination. He understood their weakness, and he knew they needed time to develop their faith. Maybe that is me and you too?

As we round that mountain on our unplanned detoured trek, do we walk through cultivating our faith? Or are we complaining, blaming, and fixated on making a way out for ourselves? Are we cultivating a new self-made plan instead of growing our mustard seed faith as we stay fixated on the uncertain course? This is hard, really hard stuff! In the process, our feet get really sore, and we stumble over the unsteady ground. We get so thirsty we can find ourselves frantically looking for our fix in every direction.

This is a reality for all of us at some point in our lives. We become very burdened and weary.

A burden is something we carry. Circling our mountain becomes heavy! New burdens seem to pile on with every corner. We desperately want to retreat to what was familiar and comfortable. We get physically tired wandering in the deep.

Weariness is something that lives inside us. Our minds fall off course. We want out, we wonder too much, and we doubt the future. We lose hope, and our faith is weakened. That combination is overwhelmingly hard.

The desert is real—and the details matter. Don't take the shortcut.

Don't we all love shortcuts though? We take them when we drive because we want to get there as fast as possible. We go on crash diets because we want to lose weight now. We have direct deposit so we can access our money immediately.

Sometimes taking shortcuts is okay, maybe even a wise thing to do. But many times, we use shortcuts in ways that compromise our integrity so we can have what we want when we want it no matter the price we will pay. But those kinds of shortcuts always cost us more in the long term. It's always best to follow God's way even if it's a long way around. There is a purpose on the long road.

Don't pull rank. Follow the lead. Let's follow blindly if necessary, but let's follow the authority that has our best in uncertain places and plans.

One of the tricks the enemy uses to capture us and bring us back to Egypt is authority issues. Our flesh pushes back when we feel pushed. We do not like to be pushed. This can be the enemy's playground with us if we allow it.

When we decide to rebel against authority because we don't agree with the direction they are taking us, or we feel that we could do a better job in a position we have not yet been promoted into, we are in effect breaking rank.

The deception is that we might think breaking rank will help us, but in fact, it harms us.

Let everyone be subject to the governing authorities, for there is no authority except that which God has established. The authorities that exist have been established by God. Consequently, whoever rebels against the authority is rebelling against what God has instituted, and those who do so will bring judgment on themselves. (Romans 13:1–2)

Let everyone be subject to the governing authorities, Now it was told the king of Egypt that the people had fled, and the heart of Pharaoh and his servants was turned against the people; and they said, "Why have we done this, that we have let Israel go from serving us?" (Exodus 14:5)

We must realize that just because we broke free from bondage for a moment, that doesn't mean the enemy won't come after us again. Why? Because he wants our services.

He wants each of us to stay bound up in spiritual darkness.

He wants us to have chronic, ungodly habits and toxic relationships and to lose our effective Christian witness by making bad choices.

He wants us to give in, give up, and lose hope. It's his ultimate game and goal, and he is good at it.

So let's be ready and be vigilant because, like Pharaoh, your adversary is not going to let you go without a fight.

I love this next part: Starve your fear, feed your faith, and push!

And Moses said to the people, "Do not be afraid. Standstill, and see the salvation of the Lord, which He will accomplish for you today. For the Egyptians whom you see today, you shall see again no more forever. The Lord will fight for you, and you shall hold your peace." (Exodus 14:13–14)

Can we stand still for a moment to see our salvation in the Lord? Fear is a liar, friends.

Many times, the fears that grip our hearts and cause us to run back into bondage instead of breaking free are also quite real.

It's the fear of dying when the doctor says you have cancer.

It's the fear of going back to that addiction because life feels too hard without it.

It's the fear of losing your home when you've been laid off for a long time.

It's the fear of divorce when your marriage has been rocky for years.

Certain fears are very real. But real or not, if we are ever going to have a final push to freedom, we must starve our fears and feed our faith.

How do we do this? To push through, we must watch what we say. Our tongue is very able to accept invitations to speak. Speech therapy for the saint is important. We need to complain less, listen more, and act with wise discernment.

> For assuredly, I say to you, whoever says to this mountain, "Be removed and be cast into the sea," and does not doubt in his heart, but believes that those things he says will be done, he will have whatever he says. Therefore, I say to you, whatever things you ask when you pray, believe that you receive them, and you will have them. (Mark 11:23–24)

Push! Let's go, weary traveler.

> Then the Lord said to Moses, "Why are you crying out to me? Tell the Israelites to move on." (Exodus 14:15)

There comes a time when our prayers need to take action, that is, an action that is consistent with the instructions given to us in the Word of God.

"I need to pray about it." We have all said it out of order because, honestly, this is our way out sometimes. It stops a conversation and allows us to hold back. Prayer will always require action, so we best be careful how quickly we spew those oh-so-familiar words.

We have to start speaking the Word, taking our stand on the promises, and breaking ties with whatever or whoever is holding us back. The truth is, breakthrough faith is more than prayer; it has corresponding actions.

When we see something behind us that we thought we left forever, we must take action and push!

That habit, that hang-up, that attitude, whatever it is that keeps us looking back to Egypt, is proof we are ready for that final push because a breakthrough is up ahead.

When all hell is breaking loose, it's proof we are in the final stages.

When the enemy is chasing us down, it's time for us to move and take the final step of faith that we have been reluctant to take. It's time to make the final push!

And like the children of Israel, as we push forward in faith, we will receive God's enabling power to enter our Promised Land!

Press on, weary traveler, in Jesus's name—amen.

Day 34

"What Did You Do with What I Gave You?"

We will be asked that question when we stand before the Lord at the end of this rat race here on earth. And a rat race it is!

Jesus says in John 17:18 (The Message), "In the same way that [the Father] gave me a mission in the world, I give them a mission in the world."

What is our assignment? What is mine for today, and what is yours? This should be on the top of our mental or tablet list of to-dos.

I believe our "to-do" lists need a title. Our list should read as Jesus said in Acts 1:8, "You will be my witnesses, in Jerusalem, in all of Judea, in Samaria, and in every part of the world."

Notice how it says "you will be," not you might be? But how? If we are a follower of Christ, we have been given gifts to use for the assignments we are given. Do we believe this? Hopefully, we do or we can because it becomes the greatest adventure of this life.

God is the very best gift giver and also has a sense of humor. I was most definitely not a good student in school. I didn't like school at all. Learning didn't come easy which to me meant it wasn't worth it. It didn't serve me well in those challenging years. But God had a plan and very productive gifts for me still. One of my gifts is teaching. It's pretty funny if you knew me back then.

Give me my camera and let me go off by myself without a plan to explore. I was a gypsy girl who liked to live free as a bird flying without a plan. I felt and still really feel comfortable in that place. But God said, "I have another gift for you." Administration is another of my giftings. Seriously! It felt so far away from who I was. Because it's so not who I was! God knows what we need and has his best for us to show the world his plan. He shapes, equips, and molds us in just the right ways to be used for his purpose and glory. What is most powerful is that he does it all through us. Our job is to say, "Yes, Lord," and follow his lead. I have been teaching for many years now. I am also a pretty good administrator. If you need it planned, organized, and carried out, I am your woman!

However, when I have some free time, you can see me with a camera in hand flying free. There is still a bit of gypsy that likes to explore her creative side.

Are you surprised by your gifting? Do you know what your gifting is? Have you said, "Yes, Lord," and celebrated with God what he is going in and through you?

If you don't know what your gifts are, you ought to explore this. It will set you on a mission that will launch you into places you never thought you could go. It truly is a great adventure.

When the Lord said he wanted us to go out in the world, notice that Jesus doesn't call us to be his salesperson or his defense attorney. We don't have to sell Jesus to others or defend him.

We love to create methods and catchy ways to get the attention of others for Jesus. Not bad, but the Lord didn't say, "Dream up some fun ways or rigid methods to memorize to teach about me." He said, "Tell them about me." The very best way for us to tell the world about Jesus is to let them see firsthand what he did to us and is doing through us. All the other really important parts of the puzzle will fall into their proper places in God's timing. He says, "Tell them about me. Share with the world my good news—the Gospel of Jesus Christ."

It's not our job to get the job done. I think with all good intentions, we lose sight of this. I know I have. We are being sent out by the messenger with his message. He comes with us and does all the finishing work. We just need to go out and be busy using our gifting to tell the world about Jesus. It's our holy assignment.

Our story might be the only Jesus they have ever seen. I have experienced this. It's powerful and very humbling to see how the Lord works out the details.

To experience this power, we must get out there wherever our assignment is for today and show them Jesus through our thoughts, our words, and our deeds.

Paul understood this privilege. It was to be walking in assignment with Christ alone.

> Paul says, "But I reckon my own life to be worth nothing to me; I only want to complete my mission and finish the work that the Lord Jesus gave me to do, which is to declare the Good News about the grace of God." (Acts 20:24 (GNT)

Lord, let it be so!

Day 35

"And What Does the LORD
Require of You??"

There are no words to express what it means to be comfortable and resting in the love of God for us, his protection, his provision, and even his presence in our lives. All make this life a beautiful display of God's love. We should stand in awe of the wonders of our King! God, what an *awe*some God. He is truly our refuge, our rescue, our joy, and our peace that surpasses words.

How often do we get all comfortable and rest in what is required of us based on God's standard for this life with him?

There is a difference between asking a question and being ready to hear the answer, isn't there? The ambiance just changed, hasn't it?

Too many people today are heading to the exit sign of the church and their faith. The numbers are staggering. It's too hard, and it's not fair. The truth is, we have bought into a big lie. The enemy is living his best life gathering all those who will bend at the slightest discomfort. A self-made world says, "I don't have to!"

Look around. How is that working for us today?

I believe it's human nature for us to want to run from and wrongly fight injustices and unfair circumstances. Our flesh doesn't have the tools and resources on its own to battle the craziness of this world. God was fully aware of this too.

149

Those who are in Christ have the tools and the resources that never run out. Yet when the going gets hard, we, too, would like to run and hide. This life doesn't come with that big red easy button.

Life in Christ has requirements and responsibilities. Why doesn't that feel all warm and fuzzy? Because it's not supposed to. It's supposed to be a holy alert to obey and respond. The world dismisses this with a loud voice today. You may have heard this verse.

He has shown you, O mortal, what is good.
And what does the Lord require of you? To act justly
and to love mercy and to walk humbly with your
God. (Micah 6:8)

What leads up to God giving his people these requirements?

In Micah 6, God is speaking and making a case against the people of Israel. The question he asks them is found in verse 3.

My people, what have I done to you? How
have I burdened you? Answer me. (Micah 6:3)

God then proceeds to remind them of what he has done and how he has redeemed them from slavery in Egypt. In consideration of all the righteous acts the Lord has done on their behalf, how should the people of Israel respond? How should we respond?

God disqualifies focusing on religious exercises. Here is how it reads in Micah 6.

My people, what have I done to you? How
have I burdened you? Answer me. (Micah 6:3)

With what shall I come before the Lord
and bow down before the exalted God?
Shall I come before him with burnt offerings,
with calves a year old?
Will the Lord be pleased with thousands of rams,
with ten thousand rivers of olive oil?

Shall I offer my firstborn for my transgression,
the fruit of my body for the sin of
my soul? (Micah 6:6–7)

What does God say to these questions?
He then makes clear the requirements.

And what does the LORD require of you? To act
justly and to love mercy and to walk humbly with
your God. (Micah 6:8)

If we are stuck in a list of rigid rules, we aren't fully walking in the requirements the Lord God has for us.

Let me share with you a very common and well-intended example:

If we are attending church every Sunday dressed in our best, sitting upright, and displaying our best behavior because we are supposed to, that is not a requirement. We are marching to man-made rules and man-made traditions. This can be hard to hear, but it's the truth.

We are to not give up meeting together. Absolutely! But if we are clouded by marching to tradition and rules not required, it creates a barrier to fully bringing our hearts to church with the urgency and desire to worship the King. We are coming up short. Marching creates a barrier to fully surrendering to the Lord. Marching according to God and his Word has never been a requirement.

There are times the Bible challenges, corrects, and rebukes. This scripture in Micah does all three. I don't know how often we think about what the Lord requires of us, but he provides an answer here in Micah. This is a great foundational message that sums up the Old Testament.

What does it mean to act justly, to love mercifully, and to walk humbly with your God? Stop here for a moment and take some time to think about this.

It demands our attention for sure. Do we have the time and courage in the requirements set before us? As the very fiber of our society has reached a critical tipping point, how do you and I as followers of Jesus Christ live out this verse in our lives every day, especially if we want to represent Christ well on the earth? What does this all really mean for us?

One thing that is clear and true about this verse is the language. God is literally saying, "I have shown you what is good to do." This leaves no room for suggestions or excuses. However, the real challenge of this verse lies in what he says after that.

The instruction is to "act justly," to "love mercifully," and to "walk humbly" with your God.

To act "justly" means you will do what is morally right or fair. Period. Let's not make more of it.

There are a lot of fingers pointing and signs marching today. There are a lot of personal pain, misunderstandings, and self-proclamation around this world today. We have so personally taken this on today that we forget where justice begins.

It begins with us, and it goes beyond the big voices. This is also not something we can only require of others. To act justly is something we must commit to doing ourselves. How are we doing?

Micah 6:8 has everything to do with character.

To be "just" is to be fair in all we do. To act justly means to be honest and tell the truth. It means we treat every person equally, hold them to the same standard, not apply a different system of fairness to one person versus another. This means we will do what is morally right even when it is not socially popular.

And that is the challenge and test. It's a very tall order. How are we doing?

To "love mercifully" implies joint loyalty and faithfulness to the love of God, which is demonstrated in a "commitment" to love others. That is a mouthful.

The word *mercy* is from the Hebrew word *hesed*, which implies a "loyal commitment" that flows out of "love."

To "love" mercifully (don't miss this) means we will respond to a situation the way God would. We will uphold his standard on earth and view every situation through this lens. It means we will love people the way he loves them and care for people the way he cares for them, especially those who are less fortunate.

Do we love mercifully, or do we try to follow the rules and do good deeds because we are supposed to? God doesn't want that. He wants our hearts fully engaged. Mercy isn't marching to religious rules. It's letting our hearts loose with love into the world and to others, especially those in a struggle.

Someone recently said to me with 100 percent good intentions, "I need to do more for the church." He is missing the purpose. Doing for the church isn't the issue; it's *why* we are doing it.

To "walk humbly" is to walk carefully before God, being mindful of how we live before him. The one who walks humbly with the Lord does so modestly and without arrogance.

To walk humbly with God means we are not only careful about our walk, but we also recognize our position is a result of God's grace and nothing else. Whoa. That right there is enough!

Our walk with God should cause us to increase in humility and decrease in our haughty ways.

When we sum up this verse, it is a call to an active faith that is lived out with actions and interactions with others and not just with words.

One Bible commentator, Kenneth L. Barker, summed up this verse: It's spot on!

Thus, this saying is not an invitation, in lieu of the gospel, to save oneself by kindly acts of equity and fairness. It was instead a call for the natural consequence of truly forgiven men and women to demonstrate the reality of their faith by living it out in the marketplace. Such living would be accompanied with acts and deeds of mercy, justice and giving of oneself for the orphan, the widow and the poor.

Amen, Lord. Let it be so with those who follow you. Lord, by your spirit, help us to act, walk, and love as you require us to.

Lord let it begin with me.

In Jesus's name.

Day 36

The Word for Today: *Learn*

Have you ever heard a word that oddly catches your attention? *Learn* was a word that stopped me recently. I sat on this word for a long while. It was odd because it had little to say to me but wouldn't leave my mind either. It took me the entire day wrestling with it.

What kind of learner are you? At the doctor's office, they ask this question. Why do they do this? I don't have a clue.

For the books, I learn by demonstration. Sit me in a corner with a book or the instruction manual on how to put something together, that thing will not turn out well. Nope, it won't have a good ending.

Now my hubby loves the manuals. Putting something together or fixing something is his thing. He loves it, and I can admire him for this.

Invite me to watch you and allow me to ask questions. Now we are getting somewhere. I will catch on quickly. How do you learn best?

I didn't like to learn in school because it was very hard for me. There weren't many alternative options back in the day for those who struggled. I think the word *learn* haunts me still because of those difficult years. Some of you might be able to relate.

If we allow the past to be our teacher, we will learn from it. Now we are talking my language. Did you learn things the hard way? I pushed the line, the buttons, and the envelope, and it taught me a lot. The school of hard knocks is where I learned so much about this life. What I have learned has launched me into who I am today. My past has become my passion.

For me, it was adding Jesus to my school of hard knocks, and the light bulb lit up. Maybe for you too. This whole life-learning thing came together very well for me. I am blessed.

Jesus knew me so well through it all. Through all the hard learning days and the school of hard knocks, he knew one day where exactly I would be. He is never late either. Jesus gathered me close, real close, one day. He took all my stuff and said, "Now this is what we are going to do. We will use all your hard stuff, and your school of hard knocks stuff too. We will use it for good. You will learn from me along the way. So pay attention to me."

Has Jesus had this talk with you too? School has been in session since, and a day doesn't go by that I don't learn a thing or two. The Holy Spirit has been the best teacher in town! We have been on many field trips. What an adventure it has been!

What does the word *learn* speak to you? Maybe you lean into learning. That is a very good journey to be on. Where has it taken you?

The way we view learning and where we land on our journey will be different for each of us. It's a matter of many choices along the way.

The root word for *learning* in my mind is truth. I have no desire to learn if it comes up short of the truth. There was a day when learning wasn't so difficult if we were truly listening. Learning came with absolutes. Right from wrong was clear. We got to choose what we would do with these absolutes.

Today, it's tricky—really tricky. The world has thrown absolutes under the bus into the ditch and has completely tried to remove them from view.

The question then becomes, What are we actually learning based on the world's definition of truth? That is pretty profound and sad.

For me and my house, we have chosen to serve the Lord, so learning has become a common occurrence in our daily life. For this, I am grateful and very blessed!

Let the word of Christ dwell in you richly,
teaching and admonishing one another in all
wisdom, singing psalms and hymns and spiritual

songs, with thankfulness in your hearts to God.
(Colossians 3:16)

Why? It's because,

All Scripture is breathed out by God and profitable for teaching, for reproof, for correction, and for training in righteousness, (2 Timothy 3:16)

The benefits:

For the word of God is living and active, sharper than any two-edged sword, piercing to the division of soul and of spirit, of joints and of marrow, and discerning the thoughts and intentions of the heart. (Hebrews 4:12)

But the Helper, the Holy Spirit, whom the Father will send in my name, he will teach you all things and bring to your remembrance all that I have said to you. (John 14:26)

I will instruct you and teach you in the way you should go; I will counsel you with my eye upon you. (Psalm 32:8)

When the Spirit of truth comes, he will guide you into all the truth, for he will not speak on his own authority, but whatever he hears he will speak, and he will declare to you the things that are to come. (John 16:13)

For the Lord gives wisdom; from his mouth come knowledge and understanding; he stores up sound wisdom for the upright; he is a shield to those who walk in integrity, guarding the paths of jus-

tice and watching over the way of his saints. Then you will understand righteousness and justice and equity, every good path. (Proverbs 2:6–9)

Who is the man who fears the Lord? Him will he instruct in the way that he should choose. (Psalm 25:12)

Call to me and I will answer you, and will tell you great and hidden things that you have not known. (Jeremiah 33:3)

Where there is no guidance, a people fall, but in an abundance of counselors there is safety. (Proverbs 11:14)

So much to learn, and so little time.

Day 37

Never

"I will never do that again!"
"Never will I put myself through this again!"
"I will never say what she said!"
"You never [fill in the blank]."
"I will never trust you."
We have all been here, and it's never a good place to be.
All of our *nevers* are a telling reaction to our fears and insecurities.
Have you ever found yourself in this place of digging in and pointing your finger? I think we all have. It's a built-in flesh defense wall we can quickly build when we feel rejection, when we feel we are left alone, or when we are not heard. The list goes on. All are symptoms of simmering fear.
Every counselor will tell us never to fight this way. We are reminded to instead begin a heated exchange with "I feel.". Once we can identify our bottom line, we realize those exclamations are irrational.
The truth is, chances are good that you and I will fall into the *nevers* again because we are sinners and fall short of God's standard instead of running to him and His Word when the struggle is real. Are you with me here?
When we bring this word *never* up against the Lord, it looks very different. God has beautiful *never promises* for us, especially in our "I-will-never" moments.

God knows just what we need when we need it.
He says the following:

> *Be strong and courageous; do not be afraid or*
> *terrified of them, for it is the LORD your God who*
> *goes with you; He will never leave you nor forsake*
> *you.* (Deuteronomy 31:6)

Keep your lives free from the love of money and be content
with what you have, for God has said,

> *Never will I leave you, never will I forsake*
> *you.* (Hebrews 13:5)

> *Now the Angel of the LORD came up from*
> *Gilgal to Bochim. And he said, "I brought you up*
> *from Egypt and led you to the land which I swore*
> *[to give] to your fathers; and I said, I will never*
> *break My covenant with you.* (Judges 2:1)

> *Cast your cares on the LORD and he will sus-*
> *tain you; he will "never" let the righteous be shaken.*
> (Psalms 55:22)

> *The LORD answered, "Could a mother forget*
> *a child who nurses at her breast? Could she fail to*
> *love an infant who came from her own body? Even*
> *if a mother could forget, I will never forget you."*
> (Isaiah 49:15)

> *Heaven and earth will pass away, but my*
> *words will never pass away.* (Mark 13:31)

> *I give them eternal life, and they shall never*
> *perish; no one will snatch them out of my hand.*
> (John 10:28)

The Lord knows all about our *nevers*. If he knows every hair on our heads, he knows our every fear and anxiety too. God is our remedy, and His Word is our rescue.

God's *never promises* will quiet our longing fearful hearts. Next time we feel backed up into a corner, when we feel rejected, frustrated, or filled with fear, how about we look at how the Lord speaks *never* into our hearts?

Let the peace of Christ fill our hearts and minds today.

Day 38

How Do You Define Creativity?

The dictionary has the definition for us: the ability to make or otherwise bring into existence something new, whether a new solution to a problem, a new method or device, or a new artistic object or form.

Are you creative? I don't think any of us can say no. We all have brought something into existence.

> Have you solved a problem with your kids? You had to be creative to do this. Kids can very tricky! (doesn't matter their age)
>
> Have you taken a recipe and tweaked it? You are creative.
>
> Have you decorated your space for a birthday or holiday or just needed to look at a different bathroom or bedroom? You are creative.
>
> Have you got sick of the clothes in your closet—the colors, the style—and changed it up with a new look? Yup, that's creative.
>
> Have you got into an argument and worked to solve it in a way that made sense to you and the other person? You are creative.
>
> Does your home speak your name and personality? You are creative.

Do you see something broken, rusty, and pretty much a piece of junk and turn it into a unique, stunning piece of junk? You are a special kind of creative.

We are all creative. I have friends who say they couldn't create something if they tried. They haven't tried hard enough. We want to think of art and crafts when we hear the word *creativity*. It is that for sure, but it's so much more.

For me, I love to make a rock tell a story! I paint pretty cool things on smooth rocks and play hide-and-seek with them. That's creative in an odd sort of way.

Did you know there here are four kinds of creativity? We will fall into one or the other or a combination.

1. *Divergent thinking.* Divergent thinking moves away from the traditional, convergent thinking, which is linear and analytical. That sounds really smart! Put simply, this person thinks outside the box and lives in the gray as opposed to black-and-white. One of my closest friends is a creative thinker like this. It makes me crazy. Everything is open-ended! Can we just land somewhere? I need an answer and prefer it to be now. She wants to explore the possibilities. Seriously! The journey is far more important to her than the landing. She has been so good for this black-and-white decision-maker. She and I will almost always come to the same place but take very different paths to get there. I love her creative thinking because it makes lots of room for empathy and reason. However, her path requires patience on my part because I tend to skip the dillydally.

I've learned a lot about people and myself spending time with my girl in the creative gray. It's not dillydallying at all. I love her. She is one of my people for this reason.

Does this creative thinker sound like you?

2. *Problem-solving.* This might be you. It is surely not me. "Let's sit down and solve this problem." What is creative about that? Absolutely nothing! "How about we sit down and think about ways to solve this problem" (insert bullet points). This thinker loves bullet points. This creative thinker makes a great teacher! Does that sound

kind of exciting to you? Does it make perfect sense to you? If so, this is your creative bend. It makes me anxious! Let's just get to the point already.

A creative problem solver is amazing. They are so patient and love to get others involved in their solving a problem. They see the big picture but take their time getting there. They discuss the options. The options are really important.

Are you a creative problem solver?

My divergent friend has brought me into this lane somewhat. The problem must be solved, right? Today, I am much more willing to look at options. We look at them, but we don't explore them. We make a decision based on them. No time for that exploration stuff.

You might be this creative person.

3. *Inspiration and imagination*. Okay, this just lit up my world! Are you with me here? This makes perfect sense to me. This speaks my language. How about you?

Inspiration is what prompts creativity. Inspiration provides the motivation that helps people believe that they can or should do something creative.

"You can do it! This person can see the problem or the project and brings passion to it. Houston is having a problem! Yes, and we are going to fix it! We think about this problem as a passageway through a dark tunnel, but there is a glimmer of light at the end. We are going in that direction. That is our option, and we head right to it. We don't need to talk about options much. We have a solution. We see it, and it's going to happen, but we are going inspired and bring our passion to it. This makes perfect sense to me, and for some, it seems like too many steps. I know there are lots of eye rolls out there, and that is okay. We all experience our creativity differently. Are you with me?

We will all fall into one of these three lanes.

4. *But God.*

In the beginning, God created the heavens and the earth. (Genesis 1:1)

Nothing compares. Talk about creative thinking in and out of the box! He had options because he created them! The pathways he took were inspired and laid out perfectly through the touch of His hand.

It is he who made the earth by his power, who established the world by his wisdom, and by his understanding stretched out the heavens. (Jeremiah 10:12)

For behold, he who forms the mountains and creates the wind, and declares to man what is his thought, who makes the morning darkness, and treads on the heights of the earth—the Lord, the God of hosts, is his name! (Amos 4:13)

O Lord, how manifold are your works! In wisdom have you made them all; the earth is full of your creatures. Here is the sea, great and wide, which teems with creatures innumerable, living things both small and great. (Psalm 104:24–25)

And then…

Then God said, "Let us make man in our image, after our likeness. And let them have dominion over the fish of the sea and over the birds of the heavens and over the livestock and over all the earth and over every creeping thing that creeps on the earth." (Genesis 1:26)

According to the grace of God given to me, like a skilled master builder I laid a foundation, and someone else is building upon it. Let each one take care how he builds upon it. (1 Corinthians 3:10)

You have an abundance of workmen: stone-cutters, masons, carpenters, and all kinds of crafts-men without number, skilled in working gold, sil-ver, bronze, and iron. Arise and work! The Lord be with you! (1 Chronicles 22:15–16)

The creator of all things created you and me in his image. This confirms we are all creative. And we have the best teacher.

We have been born of the master designer and creator of all things to live out this life being creative in all areas of our lives. I know the Lord loves to watch us grow as we explore, as we ponder our options, and as we inspire our way through tough spots.

He watches over us as we use our hands to create masterpieces from looking on over his. He paints the most beautiful landscapes for us to recreate, to explore, and to sit and ponder upon. He has opened the door very wide for our minds to be moved by means of creativity. He stands there with us as we gaze upon his beautiful creation in the hard and in the good.

The heavens proclaim the glory of God. (Psalm 19:1)

The skies display his craftsmanship.

I look up to the mountains; does my strength come from mountains? No, my strength comes from God, who made heaven, and earth, and moun-tains. (Psalms 121:1–2)

For by him all things were created, in heaven and on earth, visible and invisible, whether thrones or dominions or rulers or authorities—all things were created through him and for him. And he is before all things, and in him all things hold together. (Colossians 1:16–17)

So what about our creativity?

> *For we are his workmanship, created in Christ Jesus for good works, which God prepared beforehand, that we should walk in them.* (Ephesians 2:10)

> *For it is God who works in you, both to will and to work for his good pleasure.* (Philippians 2:13)

> *In Christ Jesus, then, I have reason to be proud of my work for God.* (Romans 15:17)

> *Equip you with everything good that you may do his will, working in us that which is pleasing in his sight, through Jesus Christ, to whom be glory forever and ever. Amen.* (Hebrews 13:21)

> *You can't use up creativity. The more you use, the more you have.* (Maya Angelou)

> *Creativity is seeing something that doesn't exist already. You need to find out how you can bring it into being and that way be a playmate with God.* (Michele Shea)

> *I have no special talent. I am only passionately curious.* (Albert Einstein)

> *Look deep into nature, and then you will understand everything better.* (Albert Einstein)

Day 39

Same Kind of Different—Together

What comes to mind when you see the word *together*?

- We are together in relationship with many people—friends, family, coworkers, and with Christ—if you are a follower. This is at the core for all of us.
- I think of putting a car together. It, too, is important. We can't drive it until at big job is done.
- I think about putting a puzzle together and the anticipation that brings for puzzle lovers. To see that beautiful picture after it has been put together is not only satisfying but also requires activity to see the result.
- I think about an army squad. Their togetherness is critical that they connect well and precisely. Their lives depend upon it.
- How about Humpty Dumpty? Have you had a Humpty Dumpty experience of being put back together again? I have! Things work much better when all the parts are working together as they should.
- How about the feeling when you've been apart from someone and that moment you are back together again?
- I think about heaven and our loved ones. One day, we will be together again.

Together is a powerful word. It comes with anticipation, and it requires action. It's about satisfaction. It is attached to longing and deep feelings. It connects to love. This word fills our days for sure.

I think to sum up *together* would be to say, together, things and people are better.

Something I am very involved with comes to mind when I see the word *together*. Each month in the summer, it is my role to reach out to my community and seek people and groups who would want to volunteer to put on a grill out for our homeless community. I am very passionate about this. It's one of my happy places for sure.

These grill outs are about juicy hamburgers and those mystery hot dogs we love to hate. But it's so much more. So much more. It's truly about two cultures, two communities colliding. For what, you might ask?

The sole purpose is the realization that "together, we are better." It's a beautiful thing to experience.

We are all the same kind of different. We just bring a different story. It's our story. If you would host or attend a grill out, you would stand in awe. This experience changes our view. So often what we once thought is now in the rearview mirror. Perspectives can change through experience.

This year we've had church groups, business people, funeral homes, families, and even a volleyball team host the grill out. A very diverse group with the same passion. All these people from every age group and lifestyle come together with the purpose to gather together.

As the groups sign up, they work hard *together* as a team to prepare for the event. They come excited and a little hesitant too. Two very different people groups will join together as one for the evening. What happens every time is that the hesitancy fades away very quickly, and what felt separate is now very together. Neither will be the same again.

Looking on, you might think there is a family reunion taking place under the park shelter number 1. Together is beautifully designed to help put back together broken things. The truth is, we are all broken. A grill-out evening opens our eyes wide to this reality of not only the brokenness of others but also our own. If we allow it, love happens in deep ways when we gather together.

The teams leave very differently from when they showed up. They get much more than what they signed up for. Together, we make brokenness better. Together, we are better.

I am a people person by nature. God designed me to be this way, so the word *together* is a really big and special word for me to focus on and enjoy today.

Who are you gathering together with today? Will you leave differently when you came?

> *Alone we can do so little; together we can do so much.* (Helen Keller)

> *None of us, including me, ever do great things. But we can all do small things with great love, and together we can do something wonderful.* (Mother Theresa)

I can't help but think about the season in my life when the Lord gathered me to himself for togetherness with him. This is the ultimate *together*. Can you recall this time in your life too? The Lord is the very best at gathering together what should be.

Have you ever thought about breaking barriers and coming together with the same kind of difference as you? You will leave a different person for sure.

Or what about the idea of living this life together with the creator of this world? The ultimate together.

It doesn't seem to matter the scenario of the idea of *together*. It's most times always better.

In Genesis 2:18, the Bible says, "And the Lord God said, it is not good that the man should be alone; I will make him a helper suitable for him" [together].

> *For just as the body is one and yet has many parts, and all the parts, though many, form*

[only] one body, so it is with Christ. [together] (1 Corinthians 12:12)

And let us consider how we may spur one another on toward love and good deeds, not giving up meeting together, as some are in the habit of doing, but encouraging one another. [together] (Hebrews 10:24–25)

Two are better than one, because they have a good reward for their toil. For if they fall, one will lift up his fellow. But woe to him who is alone when he falls and has not another to lift him up! Again, if two lie together, they keep warm, but how can one keep warm alone? And though a man might prevail against one who is alone, two will withstand him—a threefold cord is not quickly broken. [together] (Ecclesiastes 4:9–12)

And we know that for those who love God all things work together for good, for those who are called according to his purpose. [together] (Romans 8:28)

It's a great day to gather together.

Day 40

What Part?

"All the world is a stage." This is a famous quote by Shakespeare.

"And all the men and women merely players." That is pretty profound. It begs for us the question: What part are we playing?

John Calvin called the universe "God's majestic theatre." That would tell us that this life isn't just a stage we get to showcase ourselves, our stuff, our status, our trophies, and even our so-humble or not-so-humble happenings. The theater doesn't belong to us.

This brings to mind a time I spent in the Dominican Republic at a hotel under the stars one night where hotel guests from all over the world could showcase themselves in an evening of karaoke. I remember sitting there observing some really good talent, some really drunk mishaps, and some brave shy people giving it a go. It takes courage to get up there and showcase your stuff in front of a crowd sizing you up. It was a fun night to observe. I can't sing, so this stage would never be mine, but we all have one, don't we? What part we are playing is a big deal.

It's not your stage or mine at all even for a fun night of karaoke. It's God's stage where all things showcase the magnificent splendor of his surpassing wisdom, power, and love.

Since the universe is the theater for God's glory, that means the name of the *play* that has been performed since its grand debut is *Life*.

God the Father is the author of *Life*.

God the Spirit is the director.

And God the Son (Jesus) is the star actor and main character of the story.

We, at birth, have been cast as supporting actors in *Life*. We were born to play our parts. But we were not cast because of our great abilities. We get messed up here. We all do because we find our value in the doing. True, isn't it?

There are no casting calls, talent searches, or screen tests. We are *given* (keyword) a part to play with the purpose to experience the eternal joy that comes from knowing the Author/Director. This is what *Life* is all about.

Do we truly know the Director, or do we flip the script to fit our comfort and our plan for the play?

How we play out our part will determine our true purpose. Pressure? Yes, a pressure that asks us to pursue a passion toward perfection one day over self-made performances for today.

What then is our part? How do we know what to do and how are we doing?

We have the script—it's the living Word of God. It shares history. His-story—the true story of the whole world and everyone in it—gives us what we need to know in order to play our parts:

- Character descriptions
- Settings for the action
- Lines to memorize and remember
- Stage directions to follow

We are even given background information concerning the Director telling us who he is, what he is like, and where the story is going.

It's his play, and we need to know his script in order to play our part in this play called *Life*. Do we know the script, or are we stepping onto his stage fumbling with a script we all but glanced at a few times? The audience of one attends each one of our performances. How are we doing?

God doesn't write his play from a distance or behind the scenes. He has written himself into the story of the life of Jesus to walk it through with us.

The script is action-packed, filled with jaw-dropping, powerful mysteries and majesty unfolding with each scene.

The script contains five acts.

- *Act I—Creation and rebellion.* God created everything and everyone to know him and to delight in his goodness forever. The first two actors thought they could rewrite and improve upon the script. Choosing to ignore God's stage directions (commands), they sought to replace the director's authority. Hmm? Doesn't that sound familiar?

And every actor since then has followed in their footsteps. Our actions have not brought happiness and harmony, yet we keep chasing after our own way apart from the Director's script.

Peace has been broken between God and man. Selfishness and pride become the norm. This is a very sad act—one the Director doesn't want his cast to follow.

- *Act II—Israel.* The director plans to reverse the curse. He introduces the man Abraham and his descendants who would turn the rebellion into people or nations who would curse sin and bless all the world. A lot had to happen, and a lot did happen! Slavery to signs and wonders, more commands for how to play the parts. No matter what God did, people failed to obey. Tragedy followed because of their disregard for God's script. But God continued to rescue them. Sounds familiar, huh?

- *Act III—Jesus.* Enter Jesus—the main character and starring actor of *Life*. Jesus had been present all along, working behind the scenes. My God's story through me is filled with God being there when I was unaware. How about you too?

God, the Director, had to set the scene and set the stage for Jesus to make His grand entrance when the fullness of time had come. Love that! For Jesus is the Son promised to Abraham who came to put right all that we put wrong.

But how does Jesus do this? He does it by fixing the people who made everything wrong, of course. Jesus came to forgive us, to heal us, to cleanse us, to renew us, and to reconcile us to God and to one another . He took it upon himself to repair and fix all the damages that our sin has brought upon the majestic theater of God's glory. The price was big, but Jesus paid it in full by willingly laying down his life for ours and taking it up again so that we could be forgiven and set free. Amen.

This act comes with hard stuff but ends with redemption. A good end to this act.

- *Act IV—The church.* When Jesus finished playing his part, he sent his followers, those who he had fixed out into the world to continue playing their parts, telling others about the point of life and all that Jesus has done for them.

Actors are awakened to the part God has given them when they see their need for Jesus. They are given a new ear that wants to follow God's script, not out of fear or self-righteous pride but out of faith in Jesus and a deep love for him. This group of actors is called the church. It's not a building, it's the people, and Jesus made sure this would be clear.

This act has people sitting quietly pondering or at the edge of their seats in that awakened state of hearing with a new ear. Do you recall this act? I do, just like it was yesterday.

- *Act V—The end.* When Jesus went to the cross to die for all the damage (sin) the actors had committed, he posted a condemnation notice on everything evil and twisted and wrong in the world. The notice reads, "Condemned. Destruction pending."

Condemned as in this is wrong, evil, terrible, backward, foolish, destructive, and deadly. *Destruction pending* as in, "I will come again to rid the world of these things forever."

And this is how the story ends.

Jesus returns to destroy everything marked with a condemnation notice. All sickness, sadness, sin, and death are removed forever, along with everyone who insists on trying to keep those things in God's theater. The church will be resurrected, just as Jesus was, to share in God's new world together where they will spend their eternal days living the original happily ever after. The actors will finally find the happiness they longed for. It will be an eternal unchanging perfection.

This act has to cause people to get up from their seats and go and seek the Director, for they have chosen to play a part in the play, stepping onto the biggest stage in this world and focusing on their parts apart from this world.

I am so thankful today for Jesus giving me a part to play in this play titled *Life*.

It begins with a new life in him and then goes with him into all the world, giving His love away.

What part are you playing? Is the script clear to you? With your part in hand, how does it feel standing on the grandest stage ever constructed? Our hands can (will) get sweaty, we can sing or shout out, we can speak with confidence, and sometimes we will stumble too, but we were created to stand on this stage to share our parts for the world to see the beautiful love of the Director. His name is the name above all names. His name is Jesus.

This is the best act to follow.

Before we finish:
To you, my friend,

I pray that these devotions have blessed you,
have opened your heart and eyes, have convicted
and challenged you like they have me, but most
of all, I pray that you have taken a next step into
a more intimate relationship with the Lord Jesus.

Maybe you haven't ever given God a go. Maybe this book has
been a new concept for you. I am glad you have taken the time to
read it. If you are reading these words and are wondering how you
might have this freedom in Christ you've been reading about, it truly
is for you too. It does not matter where we have been, what we have
done, and even continue to do. The Lord will bring a transformation
that you can't deny. If you are wondering how this can happen, I can
help you now. It is a simple process that sends us on a lifelong adventure with the Lord.

If you are searching, you are right where you should be in this
moment. God is ready to transform your life. God wants to steal
your heart. He created you and wants you to live a surrendered life
for him.

*For God so loved the world that He gave His
only begotten Son, that whoever believes in Him
should not perish but have everlasting life.* (John
3:16)

There is some bad news that we need to deal with. We are all
sinners; we were born into it, and our sin deserves death that we cannot fix on our own. Do you believe you are a sinner?

*for all have sinned and fall short of the glory of
God...* (Romans 3:23–24)

For the wages of sin is death, but the gift of God is eternal life in Christ Jesus our Lord. (Romans 6:23)

Don't stop reading. Hope is here.

But God demonstrates His own love toward us, in that while we were still sinners, Christ died for us. (Romans 5:8)

This verse is such a gift to humanity. Jesus loved us so much that he took our sin and dealt with it. Actually, he died for it on the cross. He paid a heavy, hard price for us that we could never have paid. He created a way for us to walk with the Holy Spirit in us all the way to eternity.

Do you believe Jesus died for your sin?

If you do:

That if you confess with your mouth the Lord Jesus and believe in your heart that God has raised Him from the dead, you will be saved. (Romans 10:9)

For "whoever calls on the name of the LORD shall be saved." (Romans 10:13)

Do you believe that Jesus died and rose again for you? He did this to give you the opportunity to surrender your life to live for him. If—in the depths of your heart—you want to live this life, if you call on his name, you will be saved. If you are ready, take a couple of minutes and talk to Jesus.

"Jesus, I don't fully understand all this right now. But right now, I realize I am a sinner and want a new life with you. I believe you died on the cross for me and you rose again. I believe that you will place the Holy Spirit in me so that I can walk out my life by the power of your spirit in me. I realize I can't live this life without your love, your power, direction, and guidance. I choose today to surrender my life to you, Jesus. Take my

life and make it new. Lord, I surrender my life to you in this moment. In Jesus's name."

> *Therefore, if anyone is in Christ, he is a new creation; old things have passed away; behold, all things have become new.* (2 Corinthians 5:17)

If you have had this talk to God, welcome to the family of Christ followers! (Virtual hug!) What's next? Don't stop here. Find a Bible-believing church today. Commit to going consistently. Get a Bible and dive in! Start in the Book of John. Jesus will introduce himself to you there. Seek out a believer that can help you navigate the Bible. Talk to Jesus daily. He is officially your best friend. Take him with you each day.

Friends, this blessing is for you and me!

> *"The LORD bless you and keep you; The LORD make His face shine upon you, and be gracious to you; The LORD lift up His countenance upon you, and give you peace."* (Numbers 6:24–26)

His peace, that surpasses all our understanding. Amen.

About the Author

Linda Gottschalk, a small-town girl with a big passion, was raised in a small Midwest town where everyone knows your name. She was born to gather with people. She was a curious and spunky little girl, a wild and crazy teen, a mom of two strong beautiful daughters, and married to an amazing godly man. Her free-spirited, passionate personality launched her into a career of hairdressing. Owner of a salon for twenty-five years allowed her to unleash her passion and to give so much to others.

She was encouraged for years to write a book about where her passion has taken her. The timing was never right. It wasn't until life's unexpected interruptions shook her to the core that she knew she needed to share the peace and hope that showed up for her in the deep. Hard and difficult times can bring the best and beautiful things in the midst of messy stuff. She was given the courage and the freedom to share the real stuff that opens doors for unexpected blessings. Perhaps divine interventions.

She is a simple woman with a strong faith that has taught her many things along the way. Her desire for whomever picks up this book would be that hope and peace would reach them in a very deep place.

Printed in the USA
CPSIA information can be obtained
at www.ICGtesting.com
LVHW091536171223
766490LV00062B/1497